INDEX BY SONG TITLE

INDEX BY CD TRACK

Index by First Line

Additional Notes

Easter Rising 1916

The Easter Rising was an rebellion against British rule in Ireland and was fought over six days during Easter Week 1916.

There were three main Nationalist organisations operating in Ireland at this time: (a) *The National Volunteers* formed in September 1914, a breakaway group from the Irish Volunteers following on heated disputes as to whether Irishmen should fight in the British Army in the First World War. Its Commander-in-Chief in 1916 was Eoin McNeill, (b) *The Irish Republican Brotherhood*, a revolutionary organisation which evolved out of the Fenian movement of the 1860's. Many of the Easter Rising leaders came from its inner council including Thomas Clarke and Sean McDermott, and (c) *The Irish Citizen Army* established by The Irish Transport and General Workers Union to protect striking workers and pickets during the notorious Dublin lockout of 1913. James Connolly was the commandant of the Irish Citizen Army.

The 1916 Rising was planned by a Military Council established in 1915 by the Supreme Council of the Irish Republican Brotherhood. They collaborated with Padraig Pearse, Joseph Plunkett, Thomas McDonagh and Eamon Ceannt, all prominent members of the Volunteers. In January 1916 James Connolly was initiated into the conspiracy.

The planners feared that Eoin McNeill might not endorse the rising so they withheld the plans from him.

The leaders envisaged a general rising throughout the entire country and it certainly appeared that they had the manpower within the three organisations to realise this ambition.

However they didn't have the ammunition and weapons to achieve their desired result. The leaders looked to Germany for assistance and the German Admiralty agreed to provide a supply of weapons and ammunition for the rising. The arrangements to land the arms failed miserably.

By this time Eoin McNeill had learned of the plans and had reluctantly acquiesced to the rising. However, when he heard of the failure to land the arms and realised that the insurgents were almost without weapons and ammunition he published an order in the *Sunday Independent* cancelling all Volunteer manoeuvres scheduled for Sunday April 23rd. Most of the Volunteers obeyed this order and consequently the leaders of the rising could only muster a small portion of the potential force and it was decided to strike on Easter Monday.

The rising began on Easter Monday, April 24th, when about 1,000 Irish Volunteers and 200 members of the Irish Citizen Army seized the General Post Office and other strategic sites in Dublin. Fighting continued until the insurgents surrendered on April 29th.

The official death toll was 64 insurgents, 132 British soldiers and about 230 civilians. Extensive use of heavy artillery by the British laid waste large areas of the city centre. There were supported actions in Wexford, Galway and County Dublin and an attempted mobilisation in Cork.

The Easter Rising was a fairly unusual operation insofar as the leaders, when they learned of the fate of the German arms, fully accepted that there was absolutely no chance of success. However they decided to proceed in the hope that the display would awaken nationalist pride and revolutionary spirit among the Irish people.

There was widespread and open hostility among the Dublin population towards the insurgents during and immediately after the Rising. This sentiment changed to sympathy and then outright support as the British administration adopted a hard line and executed fifteen of the leaders along with Sir Roger Casement, who had convinced the Germans to supply weapons.

There are three ballads in this book relating to the Easter Rising:-

"Banna Strand" (page 118) laments the failure to land the German arms and ammunition in Kerry.

"The Foggy Dew" (page 38) applauds the bravery of the insurgents who mobilised and fought in the Rising.

"James Connolly" (page 2) mourns the execution of the commandant of The Irish Citizen Army.

1798 Insurrection

The rebellion of 1798 took place throughout many regions of Ireland between May 23rd (when fighting started in Dublin, Kildare and Meath) and September 23rd (the collapse of the Mayo rising).

The rebellion was planned and initiated by the Society of United Irishmen, comprised mainly of the Irish middle classes. This society was established in Belfast on October 18th, 1791, and in Dublin on November 9th.

The United Irishmen traversed religious boundaries. The majority of the members of the Belfast section was Presbyterian and the Dublin section was divided equally between Catholics and Protestants.

Inspired by the recent American and French Revolutions the objective of The United Irishmen was to remove English influence in Ireland and to reform the parliament so that English control over Irish affairs would be terminated.

The English authorities sought to destroy the United Irishmen. In May 1794 the Dublin society was suppressed, provoking the Belfast society to re-organise itself into a secret oath-bound society, planning for armed insurrection.

The 1798 Rebellion was more widespread throughout Ireland than other attempted rebellions, with action taking place in :-

1. Dublin, Kildare and Meath on the east coast. English forces killed over 300 insurgents at Tara, County Meath, and 200 at the Curragh in County Kildare. The insurgents then attempted to capture Carlow town but were heavily defeated on May 26th.

2. Eastern Ulster, including Antrim. The United Irishmen had a strong organisation in Ulster. Their main campaigns in the 1798 Rebellion centred around the towns of Antrim and Ballynahinch. The Ulster United Irishmen received less support than they had anticipated from the Antrim Catholics and due to some poor organisation and morale, and treachery, the Government forces soon regained control.

3. County Wexford where some of the fiercest fighting took place. The uprising began on May 26th. The town of Enniscorthy was captured on May 28th and Wexford town on May 30th. However on June 5th the insurgents lost over 2,000 men at the Battle of New Ross. At the Battle of Arklow on June 9th about 350 insurgents were killed. On June 21st the English forces stormed Vinegar Hill outside Enniscorthy and defeat the 20,000 strong insurgent force. Wexford town was also recaptured on that day thereby quenching the Wexford episode of the rebellion.

4. Connaught, sparked off by the landing of the French expedition at Killala Bay, County Mayo, under General Humbert on August 22nd. General Humbert was forced to surrender to the English on September 8th and the Connaught rising ended with the recapture of Killala on September 23rd.

The 1798 Rebellion is regarded as the most brutal and tragic event in Irish history. Over 30,000 Irish men and women were killed, murdered or executed in a period of eighteen weeks by the better equipped and trained English forces.

If you are ever in the town of Enniscorthy you should visit 'Aras 1798' - the '1798 Centre'. Through audio visual presentations and displays you will experience a very comprehensive overview of the rebellion. The Centre traces the 1798 Rebellion in Ireland through the use of multi-media technology, culminating in a 3D simulation of the Battle of Vinegar Hill, one of the most important battles in the rebellion.

There are five ballads in this book relating to the 1798 Rebellion:-

"Boulavogue" (page 126) celebrates the exploits of Father John Murphy, one of the leaders of the Wexford rebellion.

"The Croppy Boy" (page 134) narrates the treachery of the loyalists during the rebellion.

"Kelly From Killane" (page 96) commemorates John Kelly, one of the leaders of the attack on New Ross.

"The Rising Of The Moon" (page 28) recounts the rebellion in County Longford.

"Roddy McCorley" (page 95) laments the execution of Roddy McCorley, who took part in the rebellion in Antrim.

Thomas Moore (1779 – 1852)

Thomas Moore was born in Dublin on May 28th, 1779, son of a shoemaker. He studied in Trinity College Dublin and was a friend of Robert Emmet who led a small and abortive revolt in Dublin in 1803 and was executed as a result.

Moore was also acquainted with many of the United Irishmen and contributed to their newspaper "The Press".

Combining his compositions with popular Irish airs of the period he published his works in the famous collections known as "Irish Melodies", but now more popularly known as "Moore's Irish Melodies" or "Moore's Melodies". There were ten volumes, the first appearing in 1807 and the final one with a supplement appearing in 1834. The "Irish Melodies" were immensely popular in Ireland and Britain. The ten volumes contained 130 songs.

Moore in his "Irish Melodies" was seeking a richer and more sophisticated audience for Irish songs and the first volume was dedicated to "the Nobility and Gentry of Ireland". He was attempting to portray a more peaceful side to Irish Nationalism and his ballads are a far cry from the blood-thirsty and rebel-rousing ballads which proliferated the streets and ale houses in the early 19th century (samples of which are contained in this book – see pages 46, 66, and 112).

There were two distinctly different attitudes among Irish people towards Moore's ballads. Some considered that he had achieved more to awaken the nationalistic spirit of Irishmen than the rebel-rousing ballads more familiar to the Irish ear, while others regarded the "Irish Melodies" as whinging songs, bemoaning the downtrodden plight of Irish people, hanging from the coat-tails of the oppressor pleading for mercy.

Some of Moore's ballads were reprinted on street ballad broadsides in the middle years of the nineteenth century, particularly such songs as "Let Erin Remember" and "The Minstrel Boy".

There are five of Moore's ballads in this book:-

"Believe Me, If All Those Endearing Young Charms" (page 27)

"The Harp That Once Through Tara's Halls" (page 17)

"The Last Rose Of Summer" (page 137)

"The Meeting Of The Waters" (page 103)

"The Minstrel Boy" (page 131)

Guitar chords used in this book

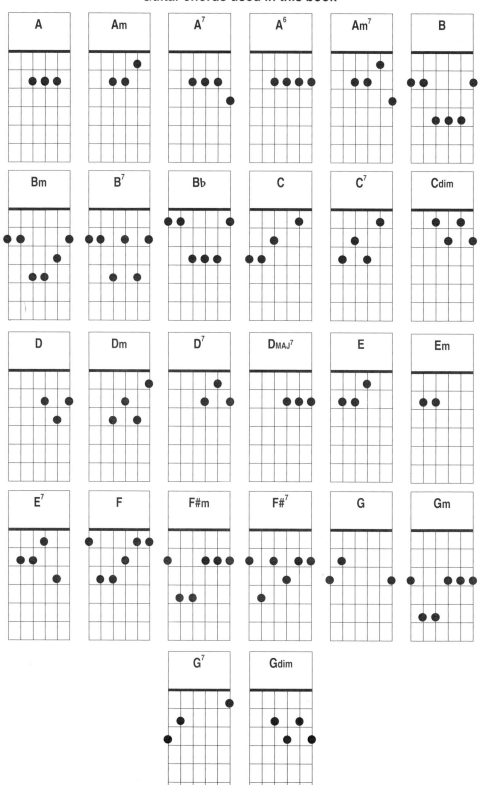

Cockles And Mussels

This ballad is also known as "Molly Malone" and is without doubt the Dublin Anthem at all sporting events, and the unofficial National Anthem among all Irish people abroad.

I believe that the earliest known version of this ballad was published in London in 1884. It was described as a comic song (!) and was attributed to James Yorkston of Scotland. It was noted as "printed with permission" of an Edinburgh firm so there must have been an earlier version.

Almost as little is known of Molly Malone as of this ballad's origin. As a fishmonger she probably lived around the Fishamble Street area of Dublin, beside Christchurch Cathedral. Fishamble Street owes its name to a medieval fish market which was held there many years ago. In those days fish was sold in markets and also by street traders who pushed their goods through the streets of Dublin on two-wheeled carts.

The word 'shamble' is an old English word for a market-place or market stall (hence, 'Fishamble' Street). These market-places are usually quite messy or cluttered. This word has filtered down through the ages and the word 'shambles' now indicates a general mess. So the next time you're told that your car, or office or hair (or life!) is 'in a complete shambles', at least you'll know where the word came from!

There is a wonderful bronze statue of the mythical Molly Malone at the junction of Grafton, Nassau and Suffolk Streets, beside Trinity College in Dublin. It is not unknown for visitors to Dublin to toss coins into the cleft of her ample bosom and make a wish!

This is a 'must learn' ballad if you wish to take part in any Irish ballad sessions anywhere in the world.

She was a fishmonger and sure 'twas no wonder
For so was her father and mother before
And they both wheeled their barrows through streets broad and narrow
Crying "Cockles and mussels, alive, alive-oh!" *Chorus*

She died of a fever and no one could save her
And that was the end of sweet Molly Malone
Now her ghost wheels her barrow through streets broad and narrow
Crying "Cockles and mussels, alive, alive-oh!" *Chorus*

James Connolly

James Connolly (1868 – 1916) was a prominent labour leader and Irish rebel. He was born of Irish immigrant parents in Edinburgh in 1868. He was invited to Dublin in 1896 to establish the Irish Socialist Republican Party but he became disillusioned with the lack of popular support and enthusiasm for his socialist-republican ideals and he moved to the USA in 1903.

Connolly was invited back to Ireland in 1910 to run the newly established Socialist Party of Ireland. He was appointed Belfast organiser of the Irish Transport & General Workers' Union. In 1911 he established The Irish Textile Workers' Union and shortly after that was jailed for his part in the 1913 'Dublin lockout'.

He was a prominent political journalist and writer. His greatest works include "Labour in Irish History" (1910) and "The Re-Conquest of Ireland" (1915).

Connolly was a fervent advocate of Irish independence but was opposed to an imperialist rebellion as he felt that ordinary working people on both sides would suffer the greatest. He hoped that Germany would provide much needed assistance in an insurrection against British Rule in Ireland. His hopes were almost achieved but for an unfortunate communications blunder at Banna Strand in County Kerry. See "Banna Strand" - page 118.

In 1916, as Commandant of the Irish Citizen Army he formed an alliance with the leaders of the Irish Republican Brotherhood for a joint insurrection against British rule in Ireland. He fought in the 1916 Easter Rising, operating from the General Post Office in O'Connell Street, the headquarters for the Rising. He was one of the signatories on the Proclamation of the Irish Republic which was read by Padraig Pearse on the steps of the GPO. His ankle was shattered by a ricochet bullet on Easter Thursday.

My grand-uncle, Risteard Gogan, was one of his stretcher bearers as the insurgents evacuated the GPO on Friday April 28th.

James Connolly was condemned to death by court-martial for his part in the Rising. He was strapped to a chair and executed by firing squad in Kilmainham Jail, Dublin on May 12th, 1916.

For further information about the Easter Rising see the Additional Notes at the front of this book.

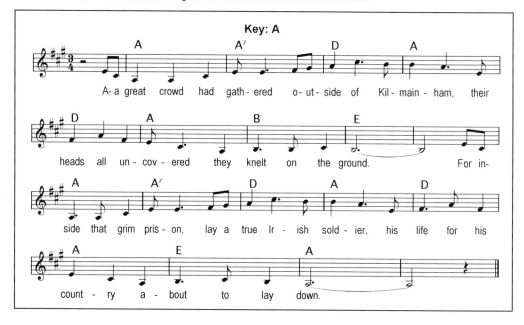

He went to his death like a true son of Erin
The firing party he bravely did face
Then the order rang out "Present arms" and "Fire!"
James Connolly fell into a ready made grave.

The black flag was hoisted, the cruel deed was over
Gone was the man who loved Ireland so well
There was many a sad heart in Dublin that morning
When they murdered James Connolly, the Irish rebel.

Many years have rolled by since the Irish Rebellion
When the guns of Britannia they loudly did speak
And the bold IRA they stood shoulder to shoulder
And the blood from their bodies flowed down Sackville Street.

The Four Courts of Dublin the English bombarded
The spirit of freedom they tried hard to quell
But above all the din came the cry "No Surrender!"
'Twas the voice of James Connolly, the Irish rebel.

~~~~~~~~~~~~~~

Sweet Carnlough Bay

Carnlough Bay is a beautiful bathing place with a crescent bay, on the coast road of County Antrim in the north-east of Ireland. It is situated at the foot of one of the smaller Antrim glens, Glencoy (one of the famous Nine Glens of Antrim),. There are several picturesque waterfalls on the stream which flows through Glencoy and this is probably the 'river' mentioned in the song. I don't know who Pat Hamill was, but he obviously ran an Inn or Tavern of some sort.

I said "My fair lassie, I surely will tell you
The road and the number of miles it will be
And if you consent I'll convey you a wee bit
And I'll show you the road to sweet Carnlough Bay".

"You turn to the right and go down by the churchyard
Cross over the river and down by the sea
We'll stop at Pat Hamill's and have a wee drop there
Just to help us along to sweet Carnlough Bay".

Here's a health to Pat Hamill, likewise the fair lassie
And to all you young lads who are listening to me
Ne'er turn your back on a bonnie wee lassie
When she's asking the road to sweet Carnlough Bay.

The Rocky Road To Dublin

In Mullingar that night I rested limbs so weary
Started by daylight next morning bright and early
Took a drop o' the pure to keep me heart from sinking
That's a Paddy's cure when e'er he's on for drinking
See the lassies smile, laughing all the while
At my daring style, 'twould set your heart a-bubblin'
They asked if I was hired, what wages I required
Till I was almost tired of the rocky road to Dublin.
Chorus

In Dublin next arrived I thought it such a pity
To be so soon deprived a view of that fine city
When I took a stroll all among the quality
Me bundle it was stole in a neat locality
Something crossed me mind, then I looked behind
No bundle could I find on me stick a-wobblin'
Enquiring for the rogue, they said my Connaught brogue
Wasn't much in vogue on the rocky road to Dublin.
Chorus

From there I got away, me spirits never failing
Landed on the quay as the ship was sailing
Captain at me roared, said that no room had he
When I jumped aboard, a cabin found for Paddy
Down among the pigs I played some funny rigs
Danced some hearty jigs, the water 'round me bubblin'
When off Holyhead I wished meself was dead
Or better far instead, on the rocky road to Dublin.
Chorus

The boys of Liverpool when we safely landed
Called meself a fool, I could no longer stand it
Blood began to boil, temper I was losing
Poor old Erin's Isle they began abusing
"Hurrah, me boys!" says I, shillelagh I let fly
Some Galway boys were by and saw I was a-hobblin'
Then with loud "Hurray!" they joined in the affray
And quickly paved the way for the rocky road to Dublin.
Chorus

Avondale

(Verses and chorus have the same melody)

'Avondale', situated near Rathdrum in County Wicklow, was the family home of Charles Stewart Parnell (1846 – 1891). The house was built in 1777 for Samuel Hayes, a barrister who represented Wicklow in the Irish House of Commons, and was originally known as 'Hayesville'. Avondale passed to the Parnell family in 1795 and it was at Avondale on June 27th 1846 that Charles Stewart Parnell was born.

Parnell was one of Ireland's greatest Nationalist political leaders. As a Home Rule Member of Parliament for County Meath (1875 – 1880) and later for County Cork (1880 – 1891), he gained a reputation for his policy of obstructing the workings of the British Parliament. He was elected President of the Irish Land League and shortly after that, Chairman of the Irish Parliamentary Party. The general election of 1885, which elected 86 Nationalist Members of Parliament, was one of his greatest achievements.

He began to lose his influence following a bout of ill health and an affair with a married woman, Kitty O'Shea. At Mrs. O'Shea's divorce proceedings Parnell was cited as the 'co-respondent' and this led to a bitter split amongst Nationalist MP's. Many of his Irish supporters turned against him and the affair destroyed his career.

In June 1891 Parnell married Kitty O'Shea. He died in Brighton in the following October.

Many of his followers believe that it was through treachery and bribery that Parnell was cited in the divorce proceedings, hence the reference to "thirty pieces of silver" in the ballad.

Avondale is now a museum to Parnell's memory with many items relating to him and his life. There are also fine pieces of furniture original to the house and the Parnell family. The house was purchased by the State in 1904 and it was at Avondale that the first silvicultural experimental plots were laid out along the lines of a continental forest garden. The house and some 214 hectares of forest park are situated about 36 miles from South Dublin and are open to the public from about March to October each year - well worth a visit.

Many ballads have been written about Charles Stewart Parnell. Another very popular one is "The Blackbird of Sweet Avondale" written by his sister, Fanny Parnell, in 1881.

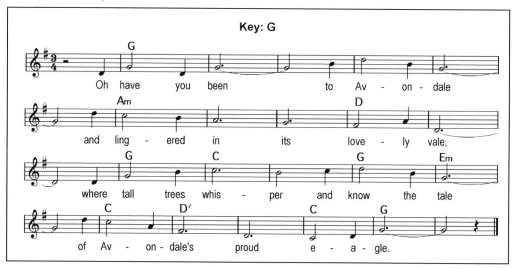

Where pride and ancient glory fade
So was the land where he was laid
Like Christ, was thirty pieces paid
For Avondale's proud eagle.

Long years that green and lovely vale
Has nursed Parnell, her proudest Gael
And cursed the land that has betrayed
Fair Avondale's proud eagle.
(Repeat first verse)

She Moved Through The Fair

This song appears in the collection "Irish Country Songs" (1909) edited by Herbert Hughes, where he states that the melody originated in County Donegal, in the north-west of Ireland. It is a very well know and haunting love song.
Herbert Hughes sets the song to a 6/4 timing, changing to 9/4 in places. However, the version I know has a 4/4 timing but it doesn't really adhere to a strict tempo and should be sung 'rubato' – without conforming to the given rhythm.
It is one of my favourite ballads in this collection, so much so that I added a verse of my own ("Twas the last time I saw her, etc").
The ballad was sung by Sinéad O'Connor to great effect in the film "Michael Collins". There is also a lovely version by the Breton harpist Alan Stivell on his album "Chemin de Terre".

She went away from me and she moved through the fair
And fondly I watched her move here and move there
And she made her way homeward with one star awake
As the swan in the evening moves over the lake.

'Twas the last time I saw her when she moved through the fair
And I gazed as the sunlight did dance through her hair
But the winds in the rushes their secret do keep
Like the waves on the shoreline, that my love's asleep.

Last night I did dream that my love she came in
And so softly she came that her feet made no din
And she laid her hand on me and smiling did say
"It will not be long love, till our wedding day".

Courtin' In The Kitchen

This Dublin ballad probably dates from the early 19th century.

"Courting" is a quaint Irish verb which means, in its broadest sense, to "get romantically involved with". It would cover every activity from holding hands, to gentle kissing, to a whole lot of other things!

There is a reference in this ballad to "Stephen's Green" which is situated in the heart of Dublin. St. Stephen's Green was originally a common in the 17th century and became a Square for the exclusive use of surrounding residents in the 18th century. It is now a beautiful 22 acre park, open to the public.

A "Repealer's Coat" was a greatcoat which sported a badge showing that the wearer was a supporter of Daniel O'Connell and his movement for the repeal of the Act of Union and the restoration of a separate Irish Parliament.

At the age of seventeen I was 'prenticed to a grocer
Not far from Stephen's Green where Miss Henri' used to go sir
Her manners were so fine; she set me heart a-twitchin'
When she asked meself to tea down in Captain Kelly's kitchen.
Chorus

Now Sunday being the day when we were to have the flare-up
I dressed meself quite gay and I frizzed and oiled me hair up
The Captain had no wife and he'd gone off a-fishin'
So we kicked up the high life out of sight down in the kitchen.
Chorus

Just as the clock struck six we sat down at the table
She handed tea and cakes and I ate what I was able
I had cakes with punch and tay till me side it got a stitch in
And the time it passed away with the courtin' in the kitchen.
Chorus

8

With me arms around her waist she slyly hinted marriage
When through the door in haste we heard Captain Kelly's carriage
Her eyes told me full well, and they were not bewitchin'
That she wished I'd get to hell, or be somewhere from that kitchen.
Chorus

She flew up off her knees, some five feet up or higher
And over head and heels threw me slap into the fire
My new Repealer's coat that I got from Mr. Mitchel
With a twenty shilling note went to blazes in the kitchen.
Chorus

I grieved to see me duds all smeared with smoke and ashes
When a tub of dirty suds right into me face she dashes
As I lay on the floor and the water she kept pitchin'
Till a footman broke the door and came chargin' to the kitchen.
Chorus

When the Captain came downstairs, though he seen me situation
Despite of all my prayers I was marched off to the station
For me they'd take no bail, though to get home I was itchin'
And I had to tell the tale of how I came into the kitchen.
Chorus

I said she did invite me but she gave a flat denial
For assault she did indict me and meself was sent for trial
She swore I robbed the house in spite of all her screechin'
And I got six months hard for me courtin' in the kitchen.
Chorus

The Mountains Of Mourne

This song was written by Percy French (1854 – 1920).

He is reputed to have written it in 1896 on a very clear day when he could see the Mountains of Mourne from the Hill of Howth in North Dublin. He sent the lyrics to his friend and colleague, Houston Collison (on the back of a postcard!), and Collison set them to the air of the song "Carrigdhoun". "Carrigdhoun" is a very popular ballad in Cork, written by the Cork merchant Denny Lane (b. 1818). and first published in 'The Nation' newspaper in 1845.

William Percy French was born on May 1st 1854 in Cloonyquin, Co. Roscommon, in the mid-west of Ireland. He was reared in comfortable circumstances, educated at upmarket English schools and eventually at Trinity College Dublin. He certainly could not be described as a model student at Trinity College for he established the record during his 'studies' for the student who took the longest time to obtain a degree!

While most of French's songs are humorous and entertaining they never ridicule, but show a warm and genuine love and affection for the Irish country folk about whom he wrote. Other songs of his include "Are Ye Right There Michael", "Sweet Marie" and "Phil The Fluther's Ball".

This song is about a lonely Irish emigrant working in London and writing a letter to his beloved in Ireland.

Apart from writing many well-remembered and popular 'drawing-room' songs Percy French was also a fine landscape painter. Today his watercolours command high prices at art auctions.

The Mountains of Mourne are situated in County Down, in the north-east of Ireland. This mountain range, the highest in Northern Ireland, is dominated by Slieve Donard, at 2,796 feet. In clear weather the Welsh and English Lake District mountains can be seen from its peaks, as well as the Isle of Arran and the Isle of Man.

The American folk-rock artist, Don McLean, recorded a fine version of this ballad.

I believe that when writing a wish you expressed
As to how the young ladies of London were dressed
Well, if you'll believe me, when asked to a ball
Sure they don't wear a top to their dresses at all
Oh I've seen them myself and you could not in truth
Say if they were bound for a ball or a bath
Don't be starting them fashions now, Mary mo chroí*
Where the Mountains of Mourne sweep down to the sea.

I've seen England's King from the top of a bus
Sure I never knew him but he means to know us
And though by the Saxon we once were oppressed
Still I cheered, God forgive me, I cheered with the rest
And now that he's visited Erin's green shore
We'll be much better friends than we've been heretofore
When we've got all we want we're as quiet as can be
Where the Mountains of Mourne sweep down to the sea.

You remember young Peter O'Loughlin, of course
Well now he is here at the head of the Force
I met him today; I was crossing the Strand
And he stopped the whole street with one wave of his hand
And as we stood talking of days that were gone
The whole population of London looked on
But for all his great powers he's wishful like me
To be back where the dark Mourne sweeps down to the sea.

There's beautiful girls here; oh never you mind
With beautiful shapes Nature never designed
And lovely complexions; all roses and cream
But O'Loughlin remarked with regard to the same
That if at those roses you venture to sip
The colour might all come away on your lip
So I'll wait for the wild rose that's waiting for me
Where the Mountains of Mourne sweep down to the sea.

*Pronounced "cree" (my beloved)

Bold Thady Quill

(The chorus is similar to the melody of the first four lines of the verse)

This ballad is popular throughout Ireland but particularly in County Cork. The air is also used in another Irish ballad, "Killeadan".
Duhallow is situated along the Cork and Kerry borders in the south of Ireland and is comprised of the ancient Baronies of Duhallow, West Muskerry and parts of East Kerry. There are three main market towns in the district - Kanturk, Millstreet and Newmarket, together with a number of small villages
Banteer is a village and townland in Duhallow about three miles from Kanturk and athletic competitions used to be held there each year. Athletes gathered from far and wide at these games which were well known and very popular. Dr. Pat O'Callaghan (1905 – 1991) who came from Duhallow, was the first athlete to win Olympic gold medals for Ireland, in 1928 and 1932, on both occasions in the hammer-throwing competition. No doubt he probably took part in the Banteer Games at some stage!
It is reputed that Thady Quill was no athlete at all, but a lazy farm worker employed by a farmer named Johnny Tom Gleeson in Ballingagree (a townland in Muskerry). The local story goes that Johnny Tom Gleeson penned these verses as a satire to Thady's laziness and inactivity. At least that's the legend anyway!
'Parnell' is a reference to Charles Stewart Parnell a nationalist and leader of the Irish Parliamentary Party who died in 1891. See "Avondale" – page 6.
'Hurling', of course, is one of our two most popular national games in Ireland (Gaelic Football being the other). It is particularly strong in the southern counties and there has been many's a passionate hurling match over the years between Cork and Tipperary!

For rambling, for roving, for football or sporting, for emptying a bowl just as fast as you'd fill
In all your days roving you'll find none so jovial as the Muskerry sportsman, the bold Thady Quill

Now Thady was famous in all sorts of places; at the athletic meeting held out in Cloughroe
He won the long jump without throwin' off his braces; goin' fifty-four feet, leppin' off from the toe
And at throwing the weight was a Dublinman foremost; but Thady outreached and exceeded him still
And 'round the whole field went the wide ringing chorus; "Here's luck to our hero, the bold Thady Quill!"
Chorus

At the great hurling match between Cork and Tipp'rary; 'twas played in the Park by the banks of the Lee
Our own darling boys were afraid of being beaten; so they sent for bold Thady to Ballinagree
He hurled the ball left and right into their faces; and showed the Tipp'rary boys learning and skill
If they came in his way he was willing to brain them; the papers were full of the praise of Thade Quill.
Chorus

In the year '91 before Parnell was taken; our Thade was outrageously breaking the peace
He got a light sentence for causing commotion; and six months hard labour for beating police
But in spite of coercion he's still agitating; ev'ry drop of his life's blood he's willing to spill
To gain for old Ireland complete liberation; till then there's no rest for the bold Thady Quill.
Chorus

At the Cork Exhibition there was a fair lady; whose fortune exceeded a million or more
But a bad constitution had ruined her completely; and medical treatment had failed o'er and o'er
"Oh mother", she said, "sure I know what'll cure me; and all my diseases most certainly kill
Give over your doctors and medical treatment; I'd rather one squeeze from the bold Thady Quill!"
Chorus

Paddy Lay Back

This ballad is an excerpt from an old capstan sea shanty which contained up to nineteen verses in some versions. The reference to 'Valiporazor' (Valiparaiso) in Chile suggests that it probably originated in Liverpool as there was much trade between the two ports. The capstan (or windlass) shanties were used for long and repetitive tasks, one of the main ones being the raising and lowering of the anchor, when the winding and unwinding was carried out by sailors walking round and round pushing at the capstan bars.
For more information on sea shanties. See "The Holy Ground" – page 132.

Now some of our fellows had been drinking; and me meself was heavy on the booze
So I sat upon me old sea chest a-thinking; I'll just turn in and have meself a snooze
Well I wished that I was in the Jolly Sailors; along with Irish Paddys drinking beer
Then I thought of what a jolly lot are sailors; and with me flipper I wiped away a tear. *Chorus*

Well when we gathered all the tugs alongside; they towed us from the wharf and out to sea
With half the crew a hanging o'er the ship's side; the bloody row that started sickened me
The bowsen he said that he couldn't savvy; the crew were speaking lingoes all galore
So the only thing the old man he could do was; just pay us sailors off and ship some more. *Chorus*

14

The Curragh Of Kildare

This beautiful ballad appears in George Petrie's collection, "Ancient Music Of Ireland" (1855), both under the present title and also that of "The Winter It Is Past".

Petrie states that a printed version of this ballad is in "The Scots Musical Museum", published in Edinburgh by the collector James Johnson in 1787 and that it also appears in the Scottish collection "Caledonian Pocket Companion" edited by James Oswald (c. 1750) under the title "The Winter It Is Past". But the ballad was also collected in Ireland by Patrick Joyce from the singing of Kate Cudmore, 'a peasant of Glenroe in the parish of Ardpatrick', County Limerick.

So the debate continues as to the origin of this song – Scotland or Ireland. Petrie believes that the Irish argument is 'decidedly the stronger'.

This ballad is reputed to be about a girl (Scottish or Irish?), heartbroken for her beloved who is an English soldier based in the Curragh military camp in Co. Kildare. She is so sorrowful that she contemplates disguising herself and enlisting in the army so that she could be with him.

The Curragh is an undulating open plain of about 5,000 acres which lies immediately east of Kildare town, about 30 miles south-east of Dublin. It derives its name from the Irish word 'An Currach' which means 'The Racecourse'. The magnificent racecourse at The Curragh is the venue for many race meetings, including the Irish Derby.

The Curragh military camp has been in existence for centuries and the British administration established a permanent military base there in 1854. A section of the Irish army is now based there.

(Note that the last verse has only two lines. These are sung to the air of the last two lines of the song).

All you that are in love and cannot it remove
I pity all the pain that you endure
For experience lets me know that your hearts are full of woe
It's a woe that no mortal can endure.

A livery I will wear and I'll straighten back my hair
In velvet so green I will appear
And it's then I will repair to the Curragh of Kildare
For it's there I'll find tidings of my dear.

The rose upon the briar and the water running free
Gives joy to the linnet and the bee
Their little hearts are blessed but mine is not at rest
For my true love is far away from me.

And it's then I will repair to the Curragh of Kildare
For it's there I'll find tidings of my dear.

The Rose Of Tralee

This song, the County Anthem of County Kerry, was written by William Pembroke Mulchinock (1820 – 1864).

The Mulchinocks were a fairly prosperous family living in Tralee and William fell in love with Mary O'Connor, the daughter of one of the family's's servants. His parents were not at all happy with this liaison and young William was quickly sent abroad for fear that his affections might grow even stronger. Following a spell in France and India William returned to Tralee. Tradition has it that on his arrival back in Tralee he saw a funeral party coming down the street. On making enquiries he was told that the deceased was his beloved Mary O'Connor, who had died from the disease of consumption. William wrote this ballad in her memory, using a local tune about the nearby Ballymullan Castle as his model.

William Mulchinock wrote many poems for various Irish journals, including "The Nation" newspaper. See "A Nation Once Again" – page 98. He left for New York in 1849 and achieved considerable success as a writer of lyrics. In 1851 he published a collection, entitled "The Ballads and Songs of W.P. Mulchinock", which oddly enough, does not contain "The Rose of Tralee".

He returned to Tralee in 1855 and died there in 1864.

The Rose of Tralee is now one of the best known and loved of all Irish ballads at home and abroad. Its popularity and endurance was assisted in no small way by a fine recording of the song by the Irish tenor John McCormack many years ago.

Tralee, the capital of County Kerry is situated near the mouth of Tralee Bay in the south-west of Ireland and is about 20 miles from Killarney. Tralee is home to a major international festival, the 'Rose of Tralee' Festival, which celebrates the beauty of the Irish Colleen and takes place every August. Tralee also has a fine racecourse and the Tralee Racing Festival is held annually at the end of August. Both Festivals are well worth a visit!

If you're in Tralee, take some time out to visit the Kerry County Museum in the centre of the town. I found it to be a most interesting museum, where interactive media and reconstructions stand side-by-side with treasures dating from the Stone and Bronze Age right up to the present day. Also in the same building you have "Kerry in Colour" – a panoramic multi-image audio-visual tour of County Kerry, and "Geraldine Tralee" where you are transported back 600 years and experience a day in the life of a medieval town, complete with sounds and smells.

Just outside the town is Blennerville Windmill – a living reminder of Ireland's rich industrial heritage. It features in the Guinness Book of Records as "the largest working windmill in these islands".

The cool shades of evening their mantles were spreading
And Mary, all smiling, sat list'ning to me
The moon through the valley her pale rays was shedding
When I won the heart of the Rose of Tralee.
Chorus

~~~~~~~~~~~~

The Harp That Once Through Tara's Halls

This is a ballad written by Thomas Moore (1779 – 1852) in which Moore uses symbolism to describe the sad state of Ireland under British rule. The harp is an ancient Irish musical instrument dating back over a thousand years. In this ballad it is used a symbol of Irish spirit and freedom.
Indeed the harp was, and still is, an important symbol representing Ireland and 'Irishness'. The harp was central to both the flag of the United Irishmen in the 1790's and the Fenian Brotherhood in the 1880's. It also featured below the crown as the official symbol of British rule in Ireland. Today the harp is to be found on the notepaper of all official Irish Government communications and is used as the Irish symbol on all Irish Euro currency coins.
The Hill of Tara is a low-lying ridge situated in County Meath, in the east of Ireland. According to ancient traditions Tara was the seat of the High Kings of Ireland who controlled the northern half of the island. None of the structures has survived – they were all built of timber in ancient times – but the earthworks and ramparts which surrounded these dwellings, together with burial mounds, are still to be clearly seen.
Apart from the legends Tara is mentioned in many old annals and writings, so it certainly seems to have played an important part in early Irish history. Nobody knows how or why Tara fell into disuse or was abandoned.
To this day the name of Tara symbolises vanished splendour and glory.
For further details about Thomas Moore and his songs see the Additional Notes at the front of this book.

No more to chiefs and ladies bright the harp of Tara swells
The chord alone that breaks at night its tale of ruin tells
The freedom now so seldom wakes the only throb she gives
Is when some heart in sorrow breaks to show that still she lives.

The Bonny Boy

This ballad is also known as "Daily Growing" and "The Bonny Boy Is Young (But Growing)" and "The Trees They Are So High". It first appeared in James Johnson's "The Scots Musical Museum" in 1792 under the title of "Lady Mary Ann" but it could be a lot older, as child marriages were common in the Middle Ages. There is speculation that the ballad may be based on the marriage in 1631 between the young Laird of Craighton to a girl several years older. He died three years after the marriage.

Oh Father dear father I think you did me wrong
For to go and get me married to one who is so young
For he is only sixteen years and I am twenty-one
And the bonny boy is young and still growing.

Oh daughter dear daughter I did not do you wrong
For to go and get you married to one who is so young
I know he'll be a match for you when I am dead and gone
Oh the bonny boy is young but he's growing.

Oh Father dear father I'll tell you what I'll do
I'll send my love to college for another year or two
And all around his college cap I'll tie a ribbon blue
Just to show the other girls that he's married.

At evening when strolling down by the college wall
You'd see the young collegiates a-playing at the ball
You'd see him in amongst them there, the fairest of them all
He's my bonny boy, he's young but he's growing.

At the early age of sixteen years he was a married man
And at the age of seventeen the father of a son
But at the age of eighteen o'er his grave the grass grew strong
Cruel death put an end to his growing.

I will make my love a shroud of the highest Holland brown
And whilst I am a-weaving it my tears they will flow down
For once I had a true love but now he's lying low
And I'll nurse his bonny boy while he's growing.

~~~~~~~~~~~~~

Nora

This song is also known as "Maggie" and was included by Sean O'Casey (with additional lyrics by himself) in his play "The Plough & the Stars". The original "Maggie" was written by the Canadian, George Johnson in 1863 to an air composed by James A. Butterfield.

The golden dewed daffodils shone, Nora and danced in the breeze on the lea
When I first said I loved only you, Nora and you said you loved only me
The birds in the trees sang their songs, Nora of happier transports to be
When I first said I loved only you, Nora and you said you loved only me.

Our hopes they have never come true, Nora; our dreams they were never to be
Since I first said I loved only you, Nora and you said you loved only me
The violets are withered and gone, Nora; I cry for the years as they flee
Since I first said I loved only you Nora and you said you loved only me.

Lanigan's Ball

Athy is a town in County Kildare, in the east of Southern Ireland, about 40 miles from Dublin.
'Punch' is a very potent alcoholic drink served from a large bowl and is very popular at Irish parties. See "The Jug of Punch" - page 104).

Meself to be sure got free invitations for all the nice colleens and boys I might ask
Just in a minute both friends and relations were dancing as merry as bees 'round a cask
There was lashings of punch, wine for the ladies; potatoes and cakes, there was bacon and tay
There were the Nolans, the Dolans, O'Gradys courting the girls and dancing away.

They were doing all kinds of nonsensical polkas all 'round the room in a whirligig
Till Julie and I soon banished their nonsense and tipped them a twist of a real Irish jig
O how that girl she got mad and we danced till we thought that the ceilings would fall
For I spent three weeks at Brook's Academy learning to dance for Lanigan's Ball. *Chorus*

The boys were all merry, the girls all hearty dancing together in couples and groups
Till an accident happened, young Terence McCarthy; he put his right leg through Miss Finnerty's hoops
The creature she fainted and called "melia murder"; called for her brothers and gathered them all
Carmody swore that he'd go no further; he'd get satisfaction at Lanigan's Ball.

In the midst of the row Miss Kerrigan fainted; her cheeks at the same time as red as a rose
Some of the boys decreed she was painted; she took a small drop too much I suppose
Her sweetheart Ned Morgan so powerful and able; when he saw his fair colleen stretched by the wall
He tore the left leg from under the table and smashed all the dishes at Lanigan's Ball. *Chorus*

Boys, O boys 'tis then there was ructions; I took a leg from young Phelim McHugh
But soon I replied to his fine introductions and kicked him a terrible hullabaloo
Old Casey the piper he nearly got strangled; they squeezed up his pipes, bellows, chanters and all
The girls in their ribbons they all got entangled and that put an end to Lanigan's Ball. *Chorus*

~~~~~~~~~~~~~~

I Know Where I'm Going

This song is included in the collection "Irish Country Songs" (1909) edited by Herbert Hughes where he states that it is an old song which originated in County Antrim (Northern Ireland).

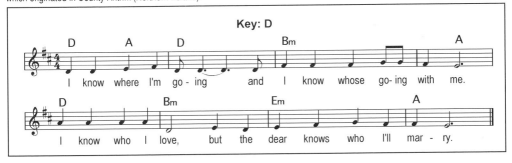

Some will say he's dark, some will say he's bonny
But the fairest of them all is my handsome noble Johnny.

I have stockings of silk, shoes of fine green leather
Combs to bind my hair and a ring for every finger.

Feather beds are soft and painted rooms are bonny
But I would leave them all to be with my darling Johnny.
(Repeat first verse)

Red Is The Rose

(Verses and chorus have the same melody)

This is a simple and charming Irish ballad sung to the air of the Scottish tune "Loch Lomond".
I added a verse of my own to this song ("But time passes on, etc").

Come over the hills my bonny Irish lass
Come over the hills to your darling
You choose the rose, love, and I will make the vow
And I'll be your true love forever.
Chorus

'Twas down by Killarney's green woodlands that we strayed
The moon and the stars they were shining
The moon shone its beams through her locks of golden hair
She swore she would love me forever.
Chorus

But time passes on and my darling girl is gone
She's gone and she's met with another
I'm full of regret but my heart will ne'er forget
That once she was truly my lover.
Chorus

It's not for the parting that my sister pains
It's not for the grief of my mother
It's all for the loss of my bonny Irish lass
That my heart is broken forever.
Chorus

My Singing Bird

The lark (or to use its official name 'Skylark', or *alauda arvensis*) is a very common bird in Ireland. It is estimated that over one million skylarks breed in Ireland each year. Their favourite habitats are the open country and coastal dunes. They make their nests on the ground, usually under clumps of tall grass. They often perch and sing on fence posts. One of the great characteristics of skylarks is their practice of flying at high altitude, especially over stubble fields where they find most of their food – cereal grain and insects.

The lark is one of the first birds to be heard in the morning in open countryside – hence it has earned the reputation as a 'symbol' of the morning and the dawn of a new day. Its continuous song consists of a constant jumble of twittering, chirping and warbling sounds, often including the imitation of other song birds.

It sings as it ascends into the heavens and hovers on fluttering wings, sometimes until it is almost out of sight.

If you want to keep your eyes open to spot skylarks their main features are sandy brown upper parts, streaked with dark brown. They have white outer tail feathers with a thin white trailing edge to their wings, visible only when open. Their underside consists of a white belly, buff breast with dark streaking heaviest on the sides. Their bills are pale, short and stubby. They have long legs, pale pink in colour with a very long claw on the hind toe.

If disturbed on the ground they will usually flutter off a short distance and land in the long grass.

There is another song in this book relating to the skylark. See "The Lark in the Morning" - page 128.

If I could lure my singing bird down from its own cosy nest
If I could catch my singing bird I'd warm it upon my breast
And in my heart my singing bird would sing itself to rest
Ah, etc. would sing itself to rest.

Finnegan's Wake

This is a very popular Dublin ballad. Tim Finnegan lived in "Watling Street" which is situated in the heart of Dublin city not far from the famous Guinness brewery at James Gate. In the ballad Tim is a builder's labourer who is rather fond of booze.
Some versions of this ballad have Tim Finnegan living in "Walkin Street" but I can't find a Walkin Street in Dublin anywhere!
James Joyce took the title of this ballad for his final book "Finnegans Wake".

One morning Tim was rather full; his head felt heavy which made him shake
He fell off the ladder and he broke his skull and they carried him home his corpse to wake
They wrapped him up in a nice clean sheet and they laid him out upon the bed
With a bottle of whiskey at his feet and a barrel of porter at his head. *Chorus*

His friends assembled at the wake and Mrs. Finnegan called for lunch
First she gave them tay and cake, then piped tobacco and brandy punch
Then the Widow Malone began to cry; such a lovely corpse she did ever see
"Yerra Tim mo bhourneen** why did you die"; "Will you hold your hour" said Molly Magee. *Chorus*

24

Then Mary Murphy took up the job; "Yerra Biddy" says she "You're wrong, I'm sure"
Then Biddy fetched her a belt in the gob and left her sprawling on the floor
Civil war did then engage; woman to woman and man to man
Shillelagh law was all the rage and a row and a ruction soon began. *Chorus*

Tim Moloney ducked his head when a bottle of whiskey flew at him
He ducked and, landing on the bed, the whiskey scattered over Tim
Well begob he revives and see how he's rising; Tim Finnegan rising in the bed
Saying "Fling your whiskey 'round like blazes! Be the thundering Jayses d'ye think I'm dead!" *Chorus*

*Booze – usually whiskey
** Pronounced "mo vourneen' (my loved one)

~~~~~~~~~~~~~~

I Never Will Marry
(Verses and chorus have the same melody)

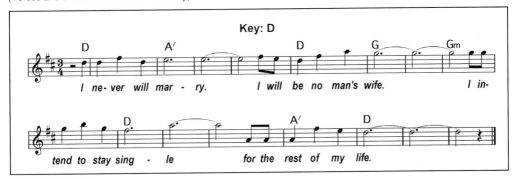

One day as I rambled down by the seashore
The wind it did whistle and the waters did roar
I heard a young maiden make a pitiful cry
She sounded so lonesome at the waters nearby. *Chorus*

"The shells in the ocean will be my death bed
May the fish in the waters swim over my head
My love's gone and left me; he's the one I adore
I never will see him, no never, no more". *Chorus*

She plunged her fair body in the water so deep
She closed her pretty blue eyes in the waters to sleep
And that lonesome maiden and her pitiful cries
Can be heard from the ocean to the heavenly skies. *Chorus*

Whiskey In The Jar

I have come across many different versions of this ballad with equally as many changes of location and character names!
This was always a very popular Irish ballad and was made even more so by a recording of a modern version of it by the Irish rock legend, Phil Lynott (now, sadly, no longer with us), and his band Thin Lizzy. It was a big hit for them back in 1973.

I counted out his money and it made a pretty penny
I put it in my pocket and I brought it home to Jenny
She sighed and she vowed that she never would deceive me
But the devil take the women for they never can be easy. *Chorus*

I went into her chamber all for to take a slumber
I dreamt of gold and jewels and for sure it was no wonder
But Jenny took my pistols and she filled them full of water
And sent for Captain Farrell to be ready for the slaughter. *Chorus*

'Twas early in the morning just before I rose to travel
The redcoats stood around the bed and likewise Captain Farrell
I then produced my pistols for she stole away my rapier
I couldn't shoot with water so a prisoner I was taken. *Chorus*

They threw me into prison, bound without a writ or bounty
For robbin' Captain Farrell near the Cork and Kerry mountains
But they couldn't take me fist so I punched and knocked the sentry
And bade no farewell to the Captain or the gentry. *Chorus*

If I could find my brother who is listed in the army
I know that he would rescue me in Cork or in Killarney
We'd set out from this place and go roving in Kilkenny
I'd be much safer there than beside my faithless Jenny. *Chorus*

Some men delight in fishing, others they like bowling
Some men like the fields or the sea that goes a-rolling
But me I take my pleasures in the juice of the barley
And not courting pretty maidens in the morning bright and early. *Chorus*

~~~~~~~~~~~~~~~~

Believe Me, If All Those Endearing Young Charms

This ballad was written in 1808 by Thomas Moore (1779 – 1852). It is believed that Moore wrote this ballad for a woman (perhaps his wife) who had suffered facial scars due to an attack of smallpox. The lyrics were set to an Irish air from the early 1800's.
For further details about Thomas Moore and his songs see the Additional Notes at the front of this book.

It is not while beauty and truth are thine own
And thy cheeks unprofaned by a tear
That the fervour and faith of a soul can be known
To which time will but make thee more dear
No, the heart that has truly loved never forgets
But as truly loves on to the close
As the sun-flower turns on her God when he sets
The same look which she turned when he rose.

The Rising Of The Moon

The lyrics for this song were written in 1865 by John Keegan Casey (1846 – 1870) to the melody of "The Wearing Of The Green" (page 74). The subject matter of the ballad is the fighting in County Longford during the 1798 Rebellion.

About 6,000 men assembled near Granard in County Longford on September 4th 1798. They were led by two brothers, Hans and Alexander Denniston, and they attacked Granard. However the attack quickly turned into a massacre and many of the insurgents fled. The English garrison of 250 Yeomen under the command of a Major Porter killed over 400 insurgents, with only two men wounded on the English side.

It is understood that Casey's original draft of the first line in the fourth verse was "There beside the Inny River…" However, not wanting to bring too much attention from the British to his own local area he changed the line to its present form.

Casey came from Milltown, Rathconrath, near the town of Mullingar in County Westmeath, in the east-midlands of Ireland. He was the son of a small farmer and was imprisoned at the age of twenty for his support of the Fenians, a revolutionary nationalist movement which was established in Ireland in the mid 19th century. When released from prison he worked as a journalist in Dublin and was a regular contributor to "The Nation" newspaper, under the pseudonym "Leo". He died as a result of a traffic accident on O'Connell Bridge in Dublin in 1870 and an enormous crowd attended his funeral.

Along with "Boulavogue" (page 126) this ballad is one of the most popular anthems of the 1798 Rebellion.

For further information about the 1798 Rebellion see the Additional Notes at the front of this book.

"Oh then tell me Sean O'Farrell where the gathering's to be"
"In the old spot by the river, right well known to you and me
One word more - for signal token, whistle up the marching tune
With your pike upon your shoulder by the rising of the moon"
By the rising of the moon, by the rising of the moon
With your pike upon your shoulder by the rising of the moon.

Out of many a mud-wall cabin eyes were watching out that night
Many a manly heart was throbbing for that blessed warning light
Murmurs passed along the valley like a banshee's lonely croon
And a thousand blades were flashing at the rising of the moon
At the rising of the moon, at the rising of the moon
And a thousand blades were flashing at the rising of the moon.

There beside that singing river that dark mass of men was seen
Far above the shining weapons hung their own beloved green
"Death to every foe and traitor! Forward! Strike the marching tune
And hurrah, me boys, for freedom! 'Tis the rising of the moon"
'Tis the rising of the moon, 'tis the rising of the moon
And hurrah, me boys, for freedom 'tis the rising of the moon.

Well they fought for dear old Ireland and full bitter was their fate
(Oh what glorious pride and sorrow fills the name of "Ninety-Eight")
Yet thank God e'en still are beating hearts in manhood's burning noon
Who would follow in their footsteps at the rising of the moon
At the rising of the moon, at the rising of the moon
Who would follow in their footsteps at the rising of the moon.

*Pronounced "voukill" (boy)

~~~~~~~~~~~~~

Twenty-One Years

I hear the train coming, 'twill be here at nine; to take me to Dartmoor to serve out my time
I look down the railway and plainly I see; you standing there waiving your goodbyes to me.

Six months have gone by, love, I wish I were dead; this cold dreary jail and a stone for my head
It's raining, it's hailing, the moon shows no light; why won't you tell me, love, why you never write?

I've counted the days, love, I've counted the nights; I've counted the footsteps, I've counted the lights
I've counted the raindrops, I've counted the stars; I've counted a million of these prison bars.

I've waited, I've trusted, I've longed for the day; a lifetime so lonely; my hair's turning grey
My thoughts are for you, love, till I'm out of my mind; for twenty-one years is a mighty long time.

Let The Grasses Grow

This ballad is also known as 'The Rare Old Mountain Dew' and is attributed to Samuel Lover (1797 – 1869). It's about that much-loved of Irish beverages – 'poitín', or poteen, also known as moonshine, or mountain dew.

The high taxation imposed on alcohol inspired many's an Irish person to resort to the illicit distillation of their own alcoholic drinks. Some of them made quite a business out of it and managed by all sorts of means to stay one step ahead of the Law.

Poitín is a colourless liquid distilled using grain, normally barley. The practice of making poitín expanded rapidly following the Revenue Act of 1779. This Act of Parliament banned small stills and imposed heavy duties on others.

The making of Poitín began to decline from 1857 onwards when the Royal Irish Constabulary assumed responsibility from the ineffectual Revenue Police for the detection of illicit stills and the prosecution of the poitín makers.

Poitín was particularly popular in rural areas and the ballad mentions Galway, a county on the west coast of Ireland. Rumour has it that poitín was (and probably still is!) extensively distilled in the Galway area. The counties of Donegal, Sligo and Leitrim are also on the west and north-west coasts of Ireland.

For another ballad about poitín, see "The Moonshiner" - page 99.

At the foot of the hill there's a neat little still where the smoke curls up to the sky
By a whiff of a smell you can plainly tell there's a poitín still nearby
Oh it fills the air with a perfume rare and betwixt both me and you
As home we roll we can drink a bowl or a bucket of mountain dew.
Chorus

Now learned men who use the pen have wrote the praises high
Of the sweet poitín from Ireland green distilled from wheat and rye
Away with pills, it'll cure all ills of Pagan, Christian or Jew
So take off your coat and grease your throat with the real old mountain dew.
Chorus

30

The Banks Of My Own Lovely Lee

This Cork anthem is a popular ballad which every self-respecting Cork person would happily sing at the drop of a hat and is affectionately known throughout Cork as 'The Banks'.

The Lee is the principle river of County Cork. It rises in Lake Gougane Barra and flows through the centre of Cork City in the south of Ireland out to the sea. The promenade of the "Mardyke" is at its centre but the elm trees are long gone. The "banks" referred to in the ballad extend westward along the Lee fields to Inishcarra and eastwards towards the harbour down the Marina to Blackrock.

And then in the springtime of laughter and song; can I ever forget the sweet hours
With the friends of my youth as we rambled along; 'mongst the green mossy banks and wild flowers
Then too, when the evening's sun sinking to rest; sheds its golden light over the sea
The maid with her lover the wild daisies pressed; on the banks of my own lovely Lee
Yes the maid with her lover wild daisies they pressed; on the banks of my own lovely Lee.

'Tis a beautiful land this dear isle of song; its gems shed their light on the world
And her faithful sons bore thro' ages of wrong; the banner St. Patrick unfurled
Oh, would I were there with the friends I love best; and my fond bosom partner with me
We'd roam thy bank over and when weary we'd rest; by thy waters, my own lovely Lee
Yes we'd roam thy banks over and when weary we'd rest; by thy waters, my own lovely Lee.

Oh what joys should be mine e're this life should decline; to seek shells on thy sea-gilded shore
While the steel-feathered eagle, oft splashing the brine; brings longing for freedom once more
Oh all that upon earth I wish for or crave; that my last crimson drop be for thee
To moisten the grass on my forefathers' grave; on the banks of my own lovely Lee
Yes to moisten the grass on my forefathers' grave; on the banks of my own lovely Lee.

O'Donnell Abú

"Abú" is an abbreviation for the Irish war cry "Go Bua!" ("To Victory!").

This ballad was written by Michael Joseph McCann (1824 – 1883), a native of County Galway. It first appeared in 'The Nation' newspaper in 1843 under the title "The Clanconnell War Song".

The subject matter of the ballad is 'Red Hugh' O'Donnell (1572 – 1602), Lord of Tirconnell from 1592, and his defeat of the English forces under Sir Conyers Clifford at Ballyshannon, Co. Donegal (north-west of Ireland) in 1597.

"Saimer" is the ancient name for the districts around Ballyshannon.

When O'Donnell was betrothed to the daughter of Hugh O'Neill , Earl of Tyrone, the English feared the establishment of a strong Irish alliance in the Northern part of Ireland and consequently O'Donnell was arrested and imprisoned in Dublin Castle. After four years, and on his second attempt, he escaped from Dublin Castle with the connivance of O'Neill. During the Nine Years War the capture of Sligo Castle allowed O'Donnell to exercise authority over most of North Connaught.

"Bonnaught" and "Gallowglass" are references to the use of mercenary troops which was widespread in Ireland during the 16th and 17th centuries.

When Spanish forces landed in Kinsale in 1601 O'Donnell marched his army down to Munster to join with them. Evading the English forces with a brilliant flanking manoeuvre at Cashel, County Tipperary, he and the Irish armies arrived successfully in Kinsale but were defeated at the Battle of Kinsale (1601). He then sailed to Spain to seek further assistance for the Irish Cause but died there.

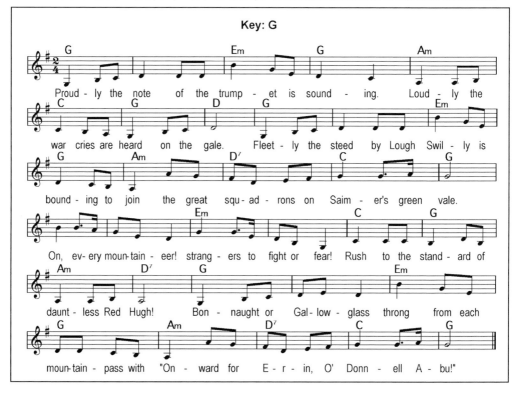

Princely O'Neill to our aid is advancing
With many a chieftain and warrior clan
A thousand proud steeds in his vanguard are prancing
'Neath Borderers brave from the banks of the Bann
Many a heart shall quail under its coat of mail
Deeply the merciless foeman shall rue
When on his ear shall ring, borne on the breeze's wing
Tir Connell's dread war cry "O'Donnell Abú!"

Wildly o'er Desmond the war-wolf is howling
Fearless the eagle sweeps over the plain
The fox in the streets of the city is prowling
And all who would scare them are banished or slain
Grasp, every stalwart hand, hackbut and battle-brand
Pay them all back the deep debt so long due
Norris and Clifford well can of Tir Connell tell
Onward to glory, O'Donnell Abú!

Sacred the cause that Clan Connell's defending
The alters we kneel at, the homes of our sires
Ruthless the ruin the foe is extending
Midnight is red with the plunderer's fires
On with O'Donnell then, fight the old fight again
Sons of Tir Connell all valiant and true
Make the false Saxon feel Erin's avenging steel
Strike for your country, O'Donnell Abú!

Monto

This great Dublin ballad was written by George Hodnett and is quite bawdy, using Dublin slang words and 'double meaning' to paint a colourful picture.

"Monto" is short for Montgomery Street which, along with Corporation Street, Railway Street and Foley Street (all located between the Custom House and O'Connell Bridge) formed one of the best known and largest red-light districts in Europe. At the beginning of the 20th century it is estimated that between 1600 and 2000 prostitutes were working at any one time in the streets. Montgomery Street was also considered at the time to be one of the worst slums in Western Europe.

The heyday of the area began in the middle of the 19th century when the district, then a fashionable group of streets, became home to two regiments of British soldiers. The women flocked to do 'business' there! This was the red-light district of gaslit, foggy and thronging streets.

The area was closed down and cleared of its night-time activities in 1925, following pressure from the citizens of Dublin.

Here are some interpretations for your better understanding of the ballad:-

"waxies" - either candle makers or those who waxed bootlaces. See "The Waxies' Dargle" - page 88; "mot" - girlfriend; "Furry Glen" - this is a small glen in the Phoenix Park. See "The Zoological Gardens" - page 69; "childer" - children; "Vicky" - Queen Victoria.

"Butcher Foster" refers to Chief Secretary Forster who introduced Coercion Acts in Ireland in the late 19th century which permitted the imprisonment of any person on the mere suspicion of being involved in criminal activity. He was very unpopular and was nicknamed 'Buckshot'.

"Invincibles" – Extremist Nationalist society with Fenian backgrounds devoted to political assassination. On May 6th 1882 The Dublin section carried out the assassination with surgical knives of the newly appointed Irish Chief Secretary Lord Frederick Cavendish and the Under-Secretary, T.H. Burke. The assassinations took place in Phoenix Park and the incident became known as 'The Phoenix Park murders'. 'Skin-the-Goat' was the nickname of James Fitzharris, the cabman who drove the Invincibles to the Park. One of the Invincibles, James Carey, was arrested and turned State's Evidence which led to the hanging of five of his comrades. Freed for his co-operation, Carey was later shot dead by an Invincible, Patrick O'Donnell, on board the ship 'The Melrose' travelling between Durban and Cape Town.

"Phoenix" – Phoenix Park; "Garda" – Irish police force; "Wearing of the Green" - well known Irish patriotic ballad (page 74).

You've heard of Butcher Foster the dirty old impostor
He took his mot and lost her up the Furry Glen
He first put on his bowler and he buttoned up his trousers
And he whistled for a growler and he said "My man
Chorus change: Take me up to Monto, etc.

You've heard the Dublin Fusiliers, the dirty old bamboozileers
They went and got their childer, one, two, three
They march them from the Linen Hall; there's one for every cannon ball
And Vicky's going to send them all o'er the sea
Chorus change: But they'll first go up to Monto, etc.

When Carey told on Skin-the-Goat, O'Donnell caught him on the boat
He wished he'd never been afloat, the dirty skite
It wasn't very sensible to tell on the Invincibles
They stuck up for the principles, day and night
Chorus change: By going up to Monto, etc.

When the Czar o' Roosha and the King o' Proosha
Landed in the Phoenix in a big balloon
They asked the Garda Band to play 'The Wearing of the Green'
But the buggers in the depot didn't know the tune
Chorus change: So they took them up to Monto, etc.

The Queen she came to call on us; she wanted to see all of us
I'm glad she didn't fall on us; she's eighteen stone
"Mister Mayor, melord", says she, "is that all you've got to show to me"
"Why no ma'am there's some more to see - póg mo thóin!"*
Chorus change: And he took her up to Monto, etc.

Pronounced "Poag mo hoan". (Kiss my a - - e!)

The Galway Races

The main Galway Racing Festival, held on the Ballybrit Racecourse just outside Galway City on the west coast of Ireland takes place towards the end of July each year. The reference to "the seventeenth of August" in the ballad is a significant one because it was on August 17th, 1869 that the Ballybrit Racecourse was opened.

The Galway Racing Festival is one of the busiest and most popular festivals in the Irish festival calendar. The ballad gives the suggestion that the festival consisted of a lot more than just the racing and this is entirely true to this day. You will notice that the sixth verse is the only one which mentions anything about the actual races themselves!

I know several people who travel to the Galway Racing Festival every year and freely admit that they wouldn't see a horse from one end of the week to the other!

A "crubeen" is a boiled pig's foot. "Wattles" are small sticks and this is a reference to a Fair Attraction whereby participants would throw sticks at a moving target (in this case the hapless Maggie) and would I presume win a prize if they hit the target. "Fenian prisoners" refers to the daring rescue of six Fenian prisoners from the penal colonies in Australia on April 17th, 1876. The prisoners were successfully brought to the USA on board the whaler 'Catalpa', much to the embarrassment of the British authorities.

"Aran" refers to the Aran Islands off the west coast of Ireland which were much more heavily populated in the 19th century than they are today. "Connemara", "New Quay" and "Clare" are all located in the west of Ireland.

Key: C

As I went down to Galway Town to seek for recreation on the seventeenth of August, me mind was elevated. There were multitudes assembled with their tickets at the station. And my eyes began to dazzle and they goin' to see the races. With me whack fol-the-do, fol-the did-del-y idle-ay.

There were passengers from Limerick town and more from Tipperary
Boys from Connemara and the Clare unmarried maidens.
People from Cork City who were loyal, true and faithful
Who brought home the Fenian prisoners from dying in foreign nations. *Chorus*

It's there you'll see the gamblers, the thimbles and the garters
The sporting Wheel-of-Fortune with the four and twenty quarters
There were others without scruple pelting wattles at poor Maggie
And her daddy well contented to be gawking at his daughter. *Chorus*

It's there you'll see the pipers and the fiddlers competing
The nimble-footed dancers a-trippin' o'er the daisies
There were others crying "Cigars and lights" and "Bills for all the races"
With the colours of the jockeys and the price and horses' ages. *Chorus*

It's there you'll see confectioners with sugar sticks and dainties
The lozenges and oranges, the lemonade and raisins
The gingerbread and spices to accommodate the ladies
And a big crubeen for threepence to be sucking while you're able. *Chorus*

It's there you'll see the jockeys and they're mounted up so stately
The pink, the blue, the orange and green, the emblems of our nation
When the bell was rung for starting all the horses seemed impatient
I thought they never stood on ground their speed was so amazing. *Chorus*

There were half a million people there from all denominations
The Catholic, the Protestant, the Jew and Presbyterian
There was yet no animosity no matter what persuasion
But sportsmen's hospitality to induce fresh acquaintance. *(Repeat chorus twice)*

~~~~~~~~~~~~~

Look At The Coffin

Look at the flowers, all bloody withered; isn't it grand boys to be bloody-well dead. *Chorus*

Look at the mourners, bloody great hypocrites; isn't it grand boys to be bloody-well dead. *Chorus*

Look at the preacher, bloody sanctimonious; isn't it grand boys to be bloody-well dead. *Chorus*

The Foggy Dew

This ballad was written by an Irish priest, Canon Charles O'Neill, as a tribute to the men and women who fought against the British in the Easter Rising of 1916.

In 1919 Canon O'Neill attended the first sitting of the Irish Parliament (Dáil Eireann). He was taken aback by the number of members at roll-call who were described as "faoi ghlas ag na Gaill" (locked up by the foreigners) and was moved by emotion to write this ballad. References in the ballad are made to Suvla Bay (Gallipoli) and Sud-el-Bar (Mesopotamia) – two battles in which many Irishmen gave their lives while serving in the British Army during the First World War.

There was an expectation among the leaders of the Rising that the British authorities would never use heavy artillery to bombard Dublin which was considered at the time to be the 'Second City' of the British Empire after London. However the insurgents were very much mistaken. Extensive use of artillery by the British laid waste large areas of the city centre – the "great big guns" referred to in the ballad.

In the ballad, reference is made to "Pearse" – Padraig Pearse, one of the leaders of the Rising; "Cathal Brugha" – one of the heroes who was badly injured during the fighting at the South Dublin Union; "Albion" – ancient name for the island of Great Britain; "Wild Geese" – a term applied to Irish patriots who were forced to flee Ireland in the 17th and 18th centuries, many of whom distinguished themselves in foreign armies; "Fenian" – a revolutionary Nationalist movement of the mid 19th century.

For further information about the Easter Rising see the Additional Notes at the front of this book.

Right proudly high in Dublin town they hoisted up the flag of war
'Twas better to die 'neath an Irish sky that at Suvle or Sud el Bar
And from the plains of Royal Meath strong men came hurrying through
While Brittania's Huns with their great big guns sailed in through the foggy dew.

Oh the night fell black and the rifles' crack made "Perfidious Albion" reel
'Mid the leaden rain seven tongues of flame did shine o'er the lines of steel
By each shining blade a prayer was said that to Ireland her sons be true
When the morning broke still the war flag shook out its folds in the foggy dew.

'Twas England made our Wild Geese flee so that small nations might be free
But their lonely graves are by Suvla's waves or the fringe of the Great North Sea
Oh had they died by Pearse's side or had fought with Cathal Brugha
Their names we would keep where the Fenians sleep 'neath the shroud of the foggy dew.

But the bravest fell and the requiem bell rang out mournfully and clear
For those who died that Easter tide in the springtime of the year
While the world did gaze with deep amaze at those fearless men, but few
Who bore the fight that Freedom's light might shine through the foggy dew.

Ah! back through the glen I rode again and my heart with grief was sore
For I parted then with valiant men whom I never will see no more
But to and fro in my dreams I go and I kneel and pray for you
For slavery fled, O glorious dead, when you fell in the foggy dew.

Bunclody

Bunclody is a town situated in County Wexford, on Ireland's east coast, about 76 miles from Dublin. At Bunclody the River Slaney joins with the River Clody. To the south-west rises Mount Leinster (2610 feet).

The town was formerly known as Newtownbarry in recognition of its patron James Barry, Sovereign of Naas, whose daughter Judith married one John Maxwell who was granted a patent for Fairs at Bunclody in 1720.

During the 1798 Rebellion insurgents under Father Kearns attacked Bunclody in an unsuccessful attempt to open communications with their comrades in Carlow and Wicklow.

The streams of Bunclody they flow down so free
By the streams of Bunclody I'm longing to be
A-drinking strong liquor in the height of my cheer
Here's a health to Bunclody and the lass I love dear.

Oh, 'tis why my love slights me as you might understand
For she has a freehold and I have no land
She has great stores of riches and a fine sum of gold
And everything fitting a house to uphold.

If I were a clerk and could write a good hand
I would write my love a letter that she would understand
For I am a young fellow that is wounded in love
Once I lived in Bunclody but now must remove.

So fare thee well father and mother, adieu
My sisters and brothers farewell unto you
I am bound for Americay my fortune to try
When I think of Bunclody I'm ready to die.

Botany Bay

(Verses and chorus have the same melody)

Botany Bay in Australia was originally known as Stingray Harbour. Located south of Sydney and its suburbs, a convict colony was established there by the English authorities in 1788. Therefore the name of Botany Bay became synonymous with penal colonies and punishment.
This ballad, however, is not the usual type of lament associated with Botany Bay and deportation. In this case the singer intends to travel to Botany Bay and make his fortune in Australia.
A 'navvy' was the term used for all labourers employed in the construction industry. The name originated at the time of the construction of artificial waterways and canals between the 17th and 19th centuries in England. These waterways were known as 'navigations'. The labourers who built these navigations were known as 'navigators', later abbreviated to 'navvy'. The name was soon applied to all construction workers.

The boss came up this morning, he says "Well Pat you know
If you don't get your navvies out I'm afraid you'll have to go"
So I asked him for my wages and demanded all my pay
For I told him straight I would emigrate to the shores of Botany Bay.
Chorus

And when I reach Australia I'll go and search for gold
There's plenty there for digging or so I have been told
Or else I'll go back to my trade and a hundred bricks I'll lay
Because I live for an eight hour shift on the shores of Botany Bay.
Chorus

Brennan On The Moor

This ballad first appeared on a broadside printed by Hay of Cork in 1850.

The central character is a highwayman called Willie Brennan who carried on his 'trade' at the beginning of the 19th century. He spent most of his time in and around the Kilworth Mountains, between the towns of Mitchelstown and Fermoy in County Cork in the south of Ireland. The main road between Dublin and Cork crosses over the Kilworth Mountains.

Highwaymen were also known as 'tories' or 'rapparees' and were regarded as champions of the poor and downtrodden. Many of these men were respectable or semi-respectable Catholic landowners who were dispossessed of their lands in the 17th century and who waged a war of revenge against the new social order. The early rapparees sheltered in the woods, mountains and boglands and waged a type of guerrilla war against the authorities and against those who has seized their lands. Rapparee activity remained widespread throughout Ireland in the troubled years immediately following the Williamite War (1689 – 1691) and continued into the 18th century in South Ulster and in parts of the south-west.

Many fine ballads have been written about these highwaymen whose daring and heroic deeds and scornful regard for the authorities and the Law endeared them to the common people. Ballads were even written about Irish rapparees who travelled abroad to carry on their trade . See "The Wild Colonial Boy" - page 60.

There was a ballad popular around the borders of Kansas and Missouri in America sung to the same air as this song and with remarkably similar words and phrases. It was entitled "Charlie Quantrell-O" and the subject of the ballad was an outlaw by the name of William Clarke Quantrill (whose nickname was 'Charlie Quantrell') who was causing a lot of trouble for the authorities around Kansas and Missouri in the 1860's.

Cashel is a town situated in County Tipperary, not far from Mitchelstown and the Kilworth Mountains.

Willie Brennan was arrested and hanged in 1804.

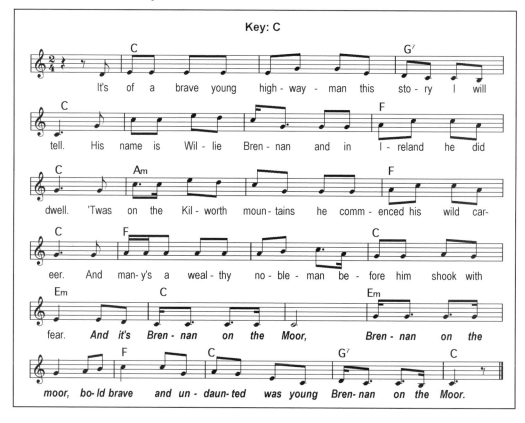

A brace of loaded pistols he carried night and day
He never robbed a poor man upon the broad highway
But what he'd taken from the rich, and nothing more or less
He always did divide it with the people in distress.
Chorus - As did Brennan on the Moor, etc.

One day upon the highway as Willie he went down
He met the Mayor of Cashel a mile outside the town
The mayor he knew his features, "I think young man" said he
"Your name is Willie Brennan, you must come along with me".
Chorus - And it's Brennan on the Moor, etc.

Now Brennan's wife had gone to town, provisions for to buy
And when she saw her Willie she began to weep and cry
She said "Hand me that tenpenny" as soon as Willie spoke
She handed him a blunderbuss from underneath her cloak.
Chorus - For young Brennan on the Moor, etc.

Then with his loaded blunderbuss the truth I will unfold
He made the mayor to tremble and robbed him of his gold
One hundred pounds was offered for his apprehension there
So he with horse and saddle to the mountains did repair.
Chorus - Did young Brennan on the Moor, etc.

Now Brennan being an outlaw and upon the mountain high
With cavalry and infantry to take him they did try
He laughed at them with scorn until at last as it was said
By a false-hearted woman he was cruelly betrayed.
Chorus - Was young Brennan on the Moor, etc.

When Brennan and his comrades they knew they were betrayed
They with the mounted cavalry a noble battle made
Then Willie's foremost finger was shot off by a ball
And Willie and his comrades they were taken one and all.
Chorus – Was young Brennan on the Moor, etc.

When Brennan heard his sentence this was his bold reply
"I owe that I did rob the rich and did the poor supply
In all the deeds that I have done I took no life away
The Lord have mercy on my soul against the Judgement Day!"
Chorus – Said young Brennan on the Moor, etc.

They put a rope around his neck, in chains he swung and died
But still they say on winter nights bold Brennan he doth ride
They say that with his blunderbuss all in the midnight chill
Across the Kilworth Mountains rides bold Willie Brennan still!
Chorus – Does young Brennan on the Moor, etc.

Johnny I Hardly Knew Ye

(Versus and chorus have the same melody)

Athy is a town in County Kildare.
This anti war ballad is very similar to another song called "When Johnny Comes Marching Home" which was written by the U.S. Union Army bandmaster Patrick Gilmore in 1863 and was a ballad glorifying army life. Nobody seem to know which song came first!
The reference to Ceylon (Sulloon) may help to date the ballad. The British occupied Ceylon from 1796 to 1948. During that period there were three rebellions for independence – 1817, which was quite serious, and two minor outbreaks in 1843 and 1848. 'Johnny' in the ballad could have been injured in one of these rebellions. Or he may have been struck down by sickness and disease which was rampant among the occupying forces in Ceylon the 19th century.

With your drums and guns and guns and drums Ha-roo, Ha-roo
With your drums and guns and guns and drums Ha-roo, Ha-roo
With your drums and guns and guns and drums the enemy nearly slew ye
My darling dear you look so queer, Johnny I hardly knew ye!

Where are your eyes that looked so mild Ha-roo, Ha-roo
Where are your eyes that looked so mild Ha-roo, Ha-roo
Where are your eyes that looked so mild when my poor heart you first beguiled
Why did you run from me and the child, Johnny I hardly knew ye. *Chorus*

Where are the legs with which you run Ha-roo, Ha-roo
Where are the legs with which you run Ha-roo, Ha-roo
Where are the legs with which you run when you went off to carry a gun
Indeed your dancing days are done, Johnny I hardly knew ye. *Chorus*

It grieved my heart to see you sail Ha-roo, Ha-roo
It grieved my heart to see you sail Ha-roo, Ha-roo
It grieved my heart to see you sail though from my heart you took leg-bail
Like a cod you're doubled up head and tail, Johnny I hardly knew ye. *Chorus*

You haven't an arm you haven't a leg Ha-roo, Ha-roo
You haven't an arm you haven't a leg Ha-roo, Ha-roo
You haven't an arm you haven't a leg you're an eyeless, noseless, chickenless egg
You'll have to be put in a bowl to beg, Johnny I hardly knew ye. *Chorus*

I'm happy for to see you home Ha-roo, Ha-roo
I'm happy for to see you home Ha-roo, Ha-roo
I'm happy for to see you home all from the island of Sulloon
So low in flesh so high in bone, Johnny I hardly knew ye. *Chorus*

But sad as it is to see you so Ha-roo, Ha-roo
But sad as it is to see you so Ha-roo, Ha-roo
But sad as it is to see you so I think of you now as an object of woe
Your Peggy'll still keep you on as her beau, Johnny I hardly knew ye. *Chorus*

~~~~~~~~~~~~~~~

Peggy Gordon

I understand that this ballad originated in Scotland.
However, it's a well known ballad in Ireland and will be heard at all decent ballad sessions!

I'm so in love and I can't deny it; my heart is smothered in my breast
It's not for you to let the world know it; a troubled mind sure it knows no rest.

I put my head to a glass of brandy; it is my fancy I do declare
For when I'm drinking I'm always thinking; and wishing Peggy Gordon was here.

I wish I was in some lonesome valley; where womankind could not be found
Where little birds sing in the branches; and every moment a different sound.
(Repeat the first verse)
(Note that four of the 'C' chords should by played slightly before the relevant note – as per the score)

The Merry Ploughboy

(Verses and chorus have the same melody)

This ballad is a parody of the English Song "The Jolly Ploughboy" which is a song in praise of the British soldier's way of life.
It is an obvious rebel song, where the singer is tired of oppression and has decided to join the I.R.A. In the English version, the singer joins the R.H.A. – the Royal Horse Artillery.
"I.R.A." refers to the Irish Republican Army. The I.R.A. evolved out of the former Irish Volunteer movement which played such a prominent role in the 1916 Easter Rising. After the foundation of Dáil Eireann in 1919 the I.R.A. began to be accepted as the armed force which would be employed to remove British rule from Ireland.
The I.R.A. fought on the anti-Treaty side in the Civil War (1922-1923) and was defeated. However the remnants of the organisation refused to recognise the subsequent Irish Free State or the legitimacy of Northern Ireland.
The I.R.A. has survived to the present day albeit in several different splinter groups and formats.

So I'm off to Dublin in the green, in the green; where the helmets glisten in the sun
Where the bayonets flash and the rifles crash; to the echo of a Thompson gun.

I'll leave aside my pick and spade, I'll leave aside my plough
I'll leave aside my old grey mare for no more I'll need them now.
Chorus

And I'll leave aside my Mary, she's the girl that I adore
And I wonder if she'll think of me when she hears the cannons roar
And when the war is over, and dear old Ireland's free
I will take her to the church to wed and a rebel's wife she'll be.
Chorus

The Bold O'Donoghue

(Verses and chorus have the same melody)

Keady is a small town in County Armagh (Northern Ireland) situated on high ground near the border with County Monaghan (Republic of Ireland).

This O'Donoghue fella seemed to fancy himself as a great catch for the ladies. Please note that all Irishmen are not like that – most of us are bashful, polite, reserved, timid and humble – even if the women do chase us around all the time!

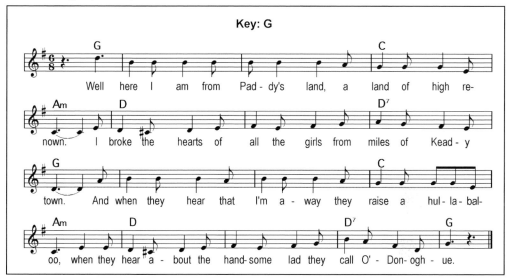

For I'm the boy to please her and I'm the boy to tease her
I'm the boy to squeeze her and I'll tell you what I'll do
I'll court her like an Irishman with me brogue and blarney too
With me rollikin, swollikin, dollikin, wollikin bold O'Donoghue.

I wish me love was a red red rose growing on yonder wall
And me to be a dewdrop and upon her brow I'd fall
Perhaps now she might think of me as a rather heavy dew
No more she'd love the handsome lad they call O'Donoghue.
Chorus

They say that Queen Victoria has a daughter fine and grand
Perhaps she'd take it into her head for to marry an Irishman
And if I could only get a chance to have a word or two
Perhaps she'd take a notion in the Bold O'Donoghue!
Chorus

The Scarriff Martyrs

This ballad concerns an incident which occurred during the War of Independence (1919 – 1921).

The War of Independence was the campaign waged by the Irish Volunteers and the Irish Republican Army against the British forces in Ireland which culminated in the signing of the Anglo-Irish Treaty and ultimately to the formation of the Irish Republic.

The Irish rebels, under Michael Collins, utilised a highly effective form of guerrilla warfare to gradually break down the effectiveness of the British occupying forces. In response to this challenge the British administration deployed regular troops together with two newly created forces, the Auxiliaries, and the 'Black and Tans".

The Black and Tans consisted mainly of British ex-soldiers and sailors and were inadequately trained and poorly disciplined. Their uniforms consisted of khaki military trousers and dark green police tunics and this odd mixture gave them their nickname.

The Black & Tans were deployed throughout the country and were notorious for their brutality (which the British authorities tacitly condoned) and for their execution of 'summary justice'.

In mid-November 1920 the Black and Tans arrested four Volunteers, Alfie Rogers, Michael Egan, Michael 'Brod' McMahon and Martin Gildea. They were taken to the bridge of Killaloe, which separates Counties Clare and Tipperary, and shot dead. The British authorities said that they were shot trying to escape but local witnesses hotly refuted this.

The four men became known as 'The Scarriff Martyrs' (Scarriff being a small town nearby to Killaloe)

The killings took place on November 16th 1920 and between 15 and 20 shots were fired at the unarmed men.

Annually in or around November 15th a wreath in memory of the four Scarriff Martyrs is placed at the monument on the bridge of Killaloe.

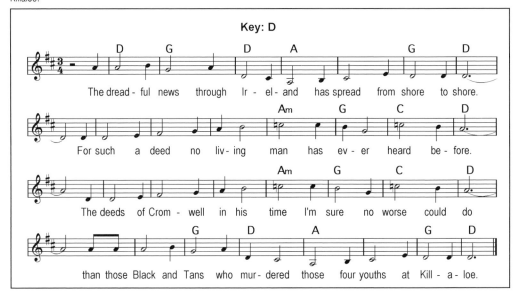

Three of the four were on the run and searched for all around
Until with this brave Egan lad from Williamstown was found
They asked him were the boys inside; in honour he proved true
Because he would not tell the pass he was shot in Killaloe.

On the fourth day of November, that day of sad renown
They were sold and traced through Galway to that house in Williamstown
They never got a fighting chance but were captured while asleep
And the way that they ill-treated them would cause your blood to creep.

They bound them tight both hands and feet with twine they could not break
And they brought them down to Killaloe by steamer on the lake
Without clergy, judge or jury upon the bridge they shot them down
And their blood flowed with the Shannon, convenient to the town.

With three days of perseverance, their bodies they let go
At ten o'clock at night their funeral passed through Ogonolloe
They were kept in Scarriff chapel for two nights and a day
Now in that place of rest they lie; kind people for them pray.

If you were at their funeral, it was an awful sight
To see the local clergy and they all dressed up in white
Such a sight as these four martyrs in one grave was never seen
For they died to save the flag they loved, the orange white and green.

Now that they are dead and gone I hope in peace they'll rest
Like all their Irish brave comrades, forever among the blessed
The day will come when all will know who sold the lives away
Of young McMahon, Rogers, valiant Egan and Gildea.

~~~~~~~~~~~~~~

A Bunch Of Thyme

This ballad has been traced as far back as the 17th century and versions can be found in Ireland and Britain.
It was a major hit in the 1970's for the folk duo, Foster & Allen.
"Thyme" in this ballad is a reference to innocence and virginity and the ballad suggests that you should never trust a sailor!

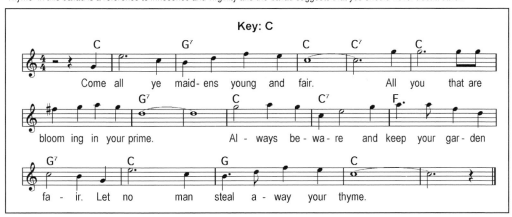

For thyme, it is a precious thing; and thyme brings all things to my mind
Thyme with all its flavours, along with all its joys; thyme brings all things to my mind.

Once I had a bunch of thyme; I thought it never would decay
Then came a lusty sailor who chanced to pass my way; he stole my bunch of thyme away.

The sailor gave to me a rose; a rose that never would decay
He gave it to me, to keep me reminded; of when he stole my thyme away.
(Repeat first verse)

Fiddlers Green

This modern song has assumed the mantle of a 'traditional ballad' due to its style and widespread popularity.
It was written by John Conolly, a ballad singer who hails from Grimsby Town.

Now Fiddlers Green is a place I hear tell
Where fishermen go if they don't go to hell
Where the skies are all clear and the dolphins do play
And the cold coast of Greenland is far far away.
Chorus

When you get to the docks and the long trip is through
And there's pubs and there's clubs and there's lassies there too
Where the girls are all pretty and the beer it is free
And there's bottles of rum hanging from every tree.
Chorus

Now I don't want a harp nor a halo, not me
Just give me a breeze and a good rolling sea
I'll play me old squeezebox as we sail along
With the wind in the rigging to sing me a song.
Chorus

The Wild Rover

This well-known ballad first appeared in print in 1904 and versions of it are to be found in Britain, Australia, Canada and the U.S.A.
In 1988 I won first prize in a talent competition on the "M.V. Orient Express" cruiser while on a cruising holiday in the Mediterranean - singing this ballad. The prize? A tee-shirt! I think I still have it somewhere.
It should have been the start of a brilliant career but, somehow, the recording contracts just didn't come in!

I went into an alehouse I used to frequent
I told the landlady my money was spent
I asked her for credit, she answered me "Nay
Such custom as yours I can have any day".
Chorus

I took out from my pocket ten sovereigns bright
And the landlady's eyes opened wide with delight
She said "I've got whiskeys and wines of the best
And the words that I spoke they were only in jest".
Chorus

I'll go home to my parents, confess what I've done
And I'll ask them to pardon their prodigal son
And if they caress me as oft times before
Sure I never will play the wild rover no more.
Chorus

Spancil Hill

This ballad of emigration and homesickness is a favourite of all folk from County Clare and, indeed, throughout Ireland.

Apparently there were eleven verses in the original song, but I only know seven of them. The ballad was written by Michael Considine, a native of Spancilhill Cross who emigrated to America in 1870 at the age of twenty.

Considine was an articulate and intelligent young man who suffered from ill-health. He worked first in Boston but later moved to California – probably to avail of the better climate. He eventually qualified as an accountant and worked all his life in America. Towards the end of his life he wrote Spancilhill and sent it back to his nephew John Considine in Ireland. He died shortly afterwards. The ballad was made famous by Robbie McMahon, a balladeer and native of Spancilhill.

Spancilhill Cross (to give it the correct name) is a crossroads situated to the east of the town of Ennis, the largest town in County Clare on the west coast of Ireland. Every year in June a week-long festival of horse, cattle and pony trading took place there. It is now held on just one day each June.

The last surviving daughter of "Tailor Quigley" died only a few years ago in Ennis.

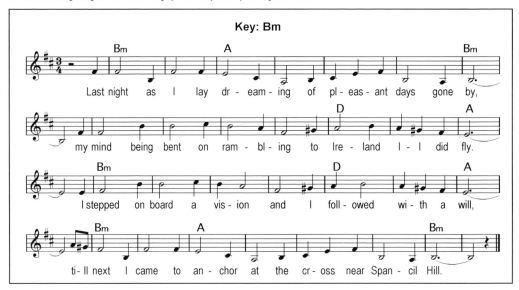

Delighted by the novelty; enchanted with the scene
Where in my early boyhood where often I had been
I thought I heard a murmur and I think I hear it still
It's the little stream of water that flows down by Spancil Hill.

To amuse a passing fancy I lay down on the ground
And all my school companions were shortly gathered around
When we were home returning we would dance with bright goodwill
To Martin Moynihan's music at the cross at Spancil Hill.

It was on the twenty-third of June; the day before the fair
When Ireland's sons and daughters and friends assembled there
The young, the old, the brave and the bold, their duty to fulfil
At the parish church at Clooney, just a mile from Spancil Hill.

I went to see my neighbours and to hear what they might say
The old ones were all dead and gone; the young ones gone away
I met the tailor Quigley; he's as bold as ever still
Sure he used to mend my britches when I lived at Spancil Hill.

I paid a flying visit to my first and only love
She's as fair as any lily and as gentle as a dove
She threw her arms around me sayin' "Johnny I love you still"
For she was a farmer's daughter and the pride of Spancil Hill.

Well I dreamt I hugged and kissed her, as in the days of yore
She said "Johnny, you're only joking!"; as many's the time before
The cock she crew in the morning; she crew both loud and shrill
And I awoke in California, many miles from Spancil Hill.

~~~~~~~~~~~~~~

Home By Bearna

This ballad originated in County Kerry, in the south-east of Ireland. It is a very popular ballad, partly I suppose because it's very easy to play – only two simple guitar chords.
Scartaglen is a townland in County Kerry not far from the border with County Cork, about 5 miles from Castleisland and nine miles from Killarney. I haven't been able to find any reference to any place called Bearna in that vicinity.

We won't go home across the fields, the big thornins could stick in your heels
We won't go home across the fields, we'll go home by Bearna
We won't go home around the glen, for fear your blood might rise again
We won't go home around the glen, but we'll go home by Bearna.

We won't go down the milk boreen, the night is bright we might be seen
We won't go down the milk boreen, but we'll go home by Bearna
We won't go home across the bog for fear we might meet Kearney's dog
We won't go home across the bog, but we'll go home by Bearna.

Boston Burglar

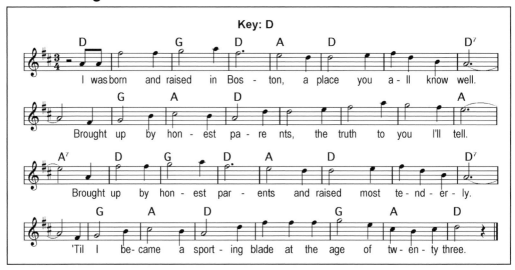

My character was taken and I was sent to jail
My parents tried to bail me out but found it all in vain
The jury found me guilty the clerk he wrote it down
The judge he passed my sentence, to be sent to Charlestown.

I see my aged father and he standing by the Bar
Likewise my aged mother and she tearing at her hair
The tearing of her old grey locks and the tears came mingled down
Saying "John my son, what have you done that you're bound for Charlestown?".

There is a girl in Boston, a place you all know well
And if e'er I get my liberty it's with her I will dwell
If e'er I get my liberty bad company I will shun
The robbing of the National Bank and the drinking of the rum.

You lads that are at liberty should keep it while you can
Don't roam the streets by night or day or break the laws of man
For if you do you're sure to rue and become a lad like me
A-serving up your youthful years in the Royal Artillery.

Dicey Riley

(Verses and chorus have the same melody)

This is a great old Dublin street ballad and I've heard many different versions of it over the years.
I'm sure that Dicey Riley (or Reilly) was a well know character in Dublin but I have no information about her.
"Heart of the rowl" is an old Dublin expression for the end of a roll of tobacco. Many years ago tobacco was sold in long lengths which were rolled up into a coil. It was commonly believed that the tail end pieces of the roll in the centre of the coil, which would be the last pieces to be sold, were more flavoursome because they would have matured the longest. Therefore the 'heart of the rowl (roll)' always signified the best.
Fitzgibbon Street is situated on the north side of Dublin's inner city, as is the area known as Summerhill.
"Sup" and "little drop" are references to booze, which Dicey Riley was evidently very fond of!

She walks along Fitzgibbon Street with an independent air
And then it's down by Summerhill where the people stop and stare
She says "It's nearly half past one, it's time I had another little one"
Ah the heart of the rowl is Dicey Riley.
Chorus

She owns a little sweet shop at the corner of the street
And every evening after school I go to wash her feet
She leaves me there to mind the shop while she nips in for another little drop
Ah the heart of the rowl is Dicey Riley.
Chorus

*Old

Skibbereen

This is a ballad about emigration and eviction.

The Great Famine occurred in Ireland between 1845 and 1849. At that time the standard staple diet of the Irish peasant was potatoes, potatoes, and more potatoes. Millions of Irish people died when the potato crops were ravaged with potato blight (*Phytophthora infestans*) over successive years. Those who could afford it boarded the notorious 'coffin ships' and the lucky ones who survived the journey started new lives in North America.

Small tenant farmers suffered eviction if they defaulted on the rent payment to their landlords, mostly English gentlemen who lived in London and employed ruthless Agents to look after their interests in Ireland. The eviction process did not take the form of merely forcibly removing the tenant farmer and his family from the cottage. It was standard for the Agent to arrive at the tenant's cottage with the Eviction Order in the company of the local Sheriff and a handful of local constabulary. The front door would be battered down, the family's belongings removed and thrown on the ground outside, and the cottage would often be burned to the ground or severely damaged. The Irish Constabulary recorded 117,000 evictions, affecting approximately 587,000 people, between 1846 and 1887. If you also take into account the 'voluntary surrenders', the number of displaced Irish peasants during that period would be considerably higher.

Skibbereen is a market town situated in West Cork in the south west of Ireland. Some of the most stunning scenery in Ireland is to be found in West Cork, along the winding roads which join the towns of Schull, Skibbereen, Ross Carbery and Clonakilty. Skibbereen is situated in what was once a very poor and somewhat bleak region. It is one of the areas that suffered most during the Great Famine. You can hear Michael Collins (Liam Neeson) reciting a verse of this ballad while in Kitty Kiernan's house, in the film "Michael Collins".

Oh son, I loved my native land with energy and pride
Until a blight came o'er my crops; my sheep and cattle died
My rent and taxes were so high I could not them redeem
And that's the cruel reason why I left old Skibbereen.

It is so well I do recall that bleak December day
The landlord and the sheriff came to drive us all away
They set my roof on fire with their cursed English spleen
And that's another reason why I left old Skibbereen.

Your mother too, God rest her soul, fell on the snowy ground
Her treasured life's possessions they lay trampled all around
She never rose but passed away, from life to mortal dream
And found a quiet resting place in dear old Skibbereen.

And you were only two years old and feeble was your frame
I could not leave you with my friends; you bore your father's name
I wrapped you in a blanket at the dead of night unseen
I heaved a sigh and bade goodbye to dear old Skibbereen.

Oh father dear the day will come when vengeance loud will call
All Irishmen with stern of faith will rally one and all
I'll be the man to lead the van beneath the flag of green
And loud and high we'll raise the cry "Remember Skibbereen!"

~~~~~~~~~~~~~

Three Score And Ten

(Verses and chorus have the same melody)

This is an old English ballad about the loss of eight fishing boats From Grimsby and Hull, wrecked in a severe storm in the North Sea in 1889. It became popular in Ireland following a recording of it some years ago by the Irish folk group The Dubliners.

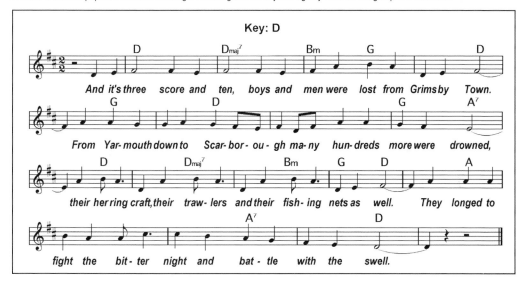

Now me thinks I see a host of gallant craft, spreading their sails a-lea
As down the Humber they did lie, bound for the cold North Sea
Me thinks I see a wee small craft, and crew with hearts so brave
They want to earn their daily bread all on the restless waves.
Chorus

October night brought such a sight, 'twas never seen before
There were masts and yards of broken spars washed up along the shore
There was many a heart of sorrow, there was many a heart so brave
There was many a true and noble lad who found a watery grave.
Chorus

The Juice Of The Barley

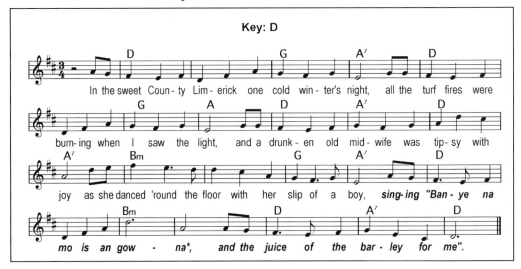

Key: D

In the sweet Coun-ty Lim-erick one cold win-ter's night, all the turf fires were
burn-ing when I saw the light, and a drunk-en old mid-wife was tip-sy with
joy as she danced 'round the floor with her slip of a boy, *sing-ing* "Ban-ye na
mo is an gow - na*, and the juice of the bar-ley for me".

Well when I was a gassoon** of eight years or so
With me turf and me primer to school I did go
To a dusty old schoolhouse without any door
Where lay the schoolmaster blind drunk on the floor. *Chorus*

At the learning I wasn't such a genius I'm thinking
But I soon bet the master entirely at drinking
Not a wake nor a wedding for five miles around
But meself in the corner was sure to be found. *Chorus*

One Sunday the priest read me out from the alter
Saying "You'll end up your days with your neck in a halter
And you'll dance a fine jig betwixt heaven and hell"
And the words they did frighten, the truth for to tell. *Chorus*

So the very next morning as the dawn it did break
I went down to the vestry the pledge for to take
And there in that room sat the priests in a bunch
'Round a big roaring fire drinking tumblers of punch. *Chorus*

Well from that day to this I have wandered alone
I'm a Jack of all Trades and a master of none
With the sky for me roof and the earth for me floor
And I'll dance out me days drinking whiskey galore. *Chorus*

*Pronounced "Ban-ya na mo iss an gow-na" (The milk of the cows and the calf)
** Young lad.

Rosin The Bow

This ballad is found in England, Scotland, North America and Ireland. It is also known as "Rosin The Beau" and the first recorded printing of it was in "English Folk Songs" (1891) edited by William Barrett.
There were many ballads composed to this air in the 19th century, including "Acres Of Clams" and Lincoln And Liberty".

Key: D

I've trav-elled this wor-ld all o-ver and now to a-noth-er must go I know that good quar-ters are wait-ing for to wel-come old Ros-in the Bow. To wel-come old Ros-in the Bow, me boys, to wel-come old Ros-in the Bow. I know that good quar-ters are wait-ing for to wel-come old Ros-in the Bow.

When I'm dead and laid out on the counter; a voice you will hear from below
Saying "Send down a hogshead of whiskey; to drink with old Rosin the Bow"
To drink with old Rosin the Bow, me lads; to drink with old Rosin the Bow
Saying "Send down a hogshead of whiskey; to drink with old Rosin the Bow".

And get a half dozen stout fellows; and stack them all up in a row
Let them drink out of half gallon bottles; to the memory of Rosin the Bow
To the memory of Rosin the Bow, me lads; to the memory of Rosin the Bow
Let them drink out of half gallon bottles; to the memory of Rosin the Bow.

Now get this half dozen stout fellows; and let them all stagger and go
And dig a great hole in the meadow; and in it put Rosin the Bow
And in it put Rosin the Bow, me lads; and in it put Rosin the Bow
And dig a great hole in the meadow; and in it put Rosin the Bow.

Now get ye a couple of bottles; put one at me head and me toe
With a diamond ring scratch out upon them; the name of old Rosin the Bow
The name of old Rosin the Bow, me lads; the name of old Rosin the Bow
With a diamond ring scratch out upon them; the name of old Rosin the Bow.

I feel that old Tyrant approaching; that cruel remorseless old foe
Let me lift up my glass in his honour; take a drink with old Rosin the Bow
Take a drink with old Rosin the Bow, me lads; take a drink with old Rosin the Bow
Let me lift up my glass in his honour; take a drink with old Rosin the Bow.

The Wild Colonial Boy

The hero of this ballad may be based on an outlaw called Jack Donahue who was a criminal transported to Australia in the early 1800's. He escaped from captivity in Australia and resumed his life of crime. He was captured and shot in 1830.

This ballad is very well known and sung throughout Ireland though the origins of the song itself are unclear. Like most old ballads there are many versions to be found. One version has the Wild Colonial Boy as 'Jack Doolan'; another as 'Jack Donahue'. Apparently there is an Australian Bush Ballad entitled 'Bold Jack Donahue' with some lines similar to the Wild Colonial Boy. There is a town in Australia called Beechwood, situated on the main road between Melbourne and Sydney, which was a major gold mining town in the last century and a Judge presided there by the name of McEvoy. So there is some truth in the ballad. But the name of the 'Wild Colonial Boy'? Who knows!

Castlemaine is a small picturesque village in County Kerry, situated on the south east coast of Ireland; but it is also a small town in Australia with a history of goldmining.

This is another example of a ballad which praises the exploits of the highwayman, or 'rapparee' as they were called in Ireland. See "Brennan on the Moor" – page 42.

At the early age of sixteen years he left his native home
And to Australia's sunny shores he was inclined to roam
He helped the poor he robbed the rich, their crops he would destroy
A terror to Australia was the Wild Colonial Boy.

For two long years this daring youth ran on his wild career
With a heart that knew no danger and a soul that felt no fear
He held the Beechwood Coach up and he robbed Judge McEvoy
Who, trembling, gave his gold up to the Wild Colonial Boy.

He bade the Judge "Good Morning" and he told him to beware
For he never robbed an honest judge who acted 'on the square'
"Yet you would rob a mother of her only pride and joy
And breed a race of outlaws like the Wild Colonial Boy".

One morning on the prairie while Jack Duggan rode along
While listening to the mocking bird a-singing out his song
Out jumped three troopers fierce and grim, Kelly, Davis and Fitzroy
Were detailed for to capture him, the Wild Colonial Boy.

"Surrender now Jack Duggan, you can see we're three to one
Surrender in our Queen's name for you are a plund'ring son"
Jack drew two pistols from his belt and glared upon Fitzroy
"I'll fight but not surrender!" cried the Wild Colonial Boy.

He fired a shot at Kelly and he brought him to the ground
He fired a shot at Davis too, who fell dead at the sound
But a bullet pierced his brave young heart from the pistol of Fitzroy
And that was how they captured him, the Wild Colonial Boy.

~~~~~~~~~~~~~~

When You Were Sweet Sixteen

This gentle love song became very popular following a recording of it by the Irish folk group The Furey Brothers in the 1970's.

Last night I dreamt I held your hand in mine; and once again you were my happy bride
I kissed you as I did in 'Auld Lang Syne'; as to the church we wandered side by side. *Chorus*

The Enniskillen Dragoon

This ballad was written by George Sigerson (1836 – 1925) who was born near Strabane in County Tyrone (Northern Ireland).
Sigerson took a degree in medicine in 1859. He taught himself Irish and took honours and a prize at a special Celtic examination in his final year in medical school.
He married and settled in Dublin. He was Professor of Botany and later of Zoology at the Catholic University Medical School and The National University of Ireland.
He wrote and edited many books, including "The Poets And Poetry Of Munster" (1860), and "Bards Of The Gael And Gall" (1897). He lived at No. 3 Clare Street in Dublin city centre and his home was a refuge and gathering-place for all those interested in Irish music and literature. He was one of the first members of the Irish Free State Seanad (Senate).
In 1911 George Sigerson inaugurated The Sigerson Cup, a trophy for a Gaelic Football Championship among Higher Level Institutions, and the Cup has been played for ever since. The Sigerson Cup is widely regarded as a breeding ground for future inter-county football players.
Dragoons originally were mounted infantrymen armed with fire-spitting muskets.

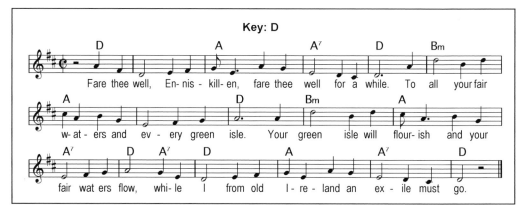

Oh they were all dressed out just like gentlemen's' sons
With their bright shining swords and new carbine guns
With their silver mounted pistols she observed them full soon
All because that she loved her Enniskillen Dragoon.

The bright sons of Mars as they stood to the right
Their armour did shine like the bright stars at night
She says "Lovely Willie, you've enlisted too soon
To serve as a Royal Enniskillen Dragoon".

"Oh beautiful Flora your pardon I crave
From now and forever I will act as your slave
Your parents insult you both morning and noon
For fear you should wed your Enniskillen Dragoon".

"Oh now, dearest Willie you should mind what you say
Until I'm of age my parents I must obey
But when you're leaving Ireland they will surely change their tune
Saying 'The Lord be he with you Enniskillen Dragoon' ".

Farewell Enniskillen fare thee well for a while
And all around the borders of Erin's green isle
And when the wars are over I'll return in full bloom
And they'll all welcome home their Enniskillen Dragoon.

Now the war is over they've returned home at last
The regiment's in Dublin and Willie got a pass
Last Sunday they were married and bold Willie was the groom
And now she enjoys her Enniskillen Dragoon.

~~~~~~~~~~~~~~

The Butcher Boy

Key: D

In Dublin Town where I did dwell, A butcher boy
I loved so well. He courted me by night and day.
He stole from me my heart a - way.

I wish my baby it was born, and smiling on its daddy's knee
And my poor body to be dead and gone, with the long green grass growing over me.

I'll go upstairs and make my bed; "What's there to do?" my mother said
My mother she has followed me, and saying "what's to come of thee?"
Chorus

"Oh mother dear you little know, my pain and sorrow and my woe
Go get a chair and sit me down; with pen and ink I'll write it down".

Her father he came home that night, enquiring for his heart's delight
He went upstairs the door he broke, and found her hanging by a rope.
Chorus

He took a knife and cut her down, and in her bosom these lines he found
"Oh what a foolish girl was I, to give my heart to a butcher boy".

"Go dig my grave both wide and deep; put a marble stone at my head and feet
And in the middle a turtle dove, so the world might know I died for love.
Chorus

The Banks Of The Roses

This ballad dates from the end of the 18th century and is thought to have originated in County Limerick.
There are many versions of this ballad to be found and in some of them Johnny takes his lover to a cave and murders her, burying her body on the Banks of the Roses.

"When I was just a young girl I heard my father say
'I'd sooner see you dead, my girl, and buried in the clay
Rather than be married to a roving runaway
On the lovely sweet banks of the roses' ".

Oh well now I am a runaway and sure I'll let you know
That I can take a bottle and drink with anyone
If her father doesn't like me he can keep his daughter home
Then young Johnny will go roving with another.

If I ever get wedded 'twill be in the month of May
When the leaves they are green and the meadows they are gay
And me and my true love will sit and sport and play
By the lovely sweet banks of the roses.

Arthur McBride

This old anti-recruitment ballad was probably written during the Napoleonic Wars (1792 – 1815), hence the reference to France. It is believed that the song originated in Ireland but versions of it are also known in England and Scotland. The song was collected by W.P. Joyce in the 1840's and around the same time the ballad collector George Petrie received a version from Donegal.

It was the practice of Recruiting Sergeants in the British Army to tempt young, impressionable and destitute men to enlist by offering them the immediate payment of a shilling. They were also bombarded with romantic descriptions of a soldier's life. Many succumbed to the temptation, much to their later regret. The practice was known as 'taking the King's shilling' and was discontinued in 1879.

The Recruiting Sergeant was one of the most hated persons in Ireland. For many of the destitute Irish peasants the only hope of escaping starvation was to join the British army and thus fight for a power which they despised. Foot soldiers were subjected to terrible conditions in the British Army and discipline was strict and harsh. The minimum punishment for misdemeanours was 25 lashes of the cat-o'-nine-tails and the maximum was 1500 lashes! Anti-recruitment ballads became very popular throughout the 19th and early 20th centuries with such songs as ""Johnny I Hardly Knew Ye" (page 44), "Mrs. McGrath" and "The Kerry Recruit".

I have come across two fine, and very different, versions of this ballad recorded by Irish artists. One was recorded by the folk group Planxty on an album called "Planxty" - very similar to this version. The other version was recorded by Paul Brady on the album "Andy Irvine & Paul Brady". Both recordings were made in the 1970's and are available today on CD.

He said "My young fellows if you will enlist; a guinea you quickly will have in your fist
And besides a whole crown for to kick up the dust; and drink the King's health till the morning"
Had we been such fools as to take the advance; with the wee bit of money we'd have to run chance
"For you'd think it no scruples to send us to France; where we would be killed in the morning".

He said "My young fellows if I hear but one word; I instantly now will out with my sword
And into your bodies as strength will afford; so now my gay devils take warning"
But Arthur and I we soon took the odds; and gave them no time for to draw out their blades
Our trusty shillelaghs came over their heads; and paid them right smart in the morning.

As for the wee drummer we rifled his pouch; and we made a football of his rowdy-dow-dow
And into the ocean to rock and to roll; and bade him a tedious returning
As for the old rapier that hung by his side; we flung it as far as we could in the tide
"To the devil I pitch you" said Arthur McBride; "to temper your steel in the morning".

Follow Me Up To Carlow

This is a rousing and gory ballad, reputed to have been written by Patrick J. McCall (1861 – 1919). The ballad celebrates the victory of Fiach McHugh O'Byrne (c. 1544 – 1597) over the English forces at Glenmalure in 1580.

Fiach McHugh O'Byrne was the leader of the O'Byrne clan in Co. Wicklow and was a major thorn in England's side.

In 1580 the newly arrived Lord Deputy Leonard Grey decided to confront O'Byrne and his ally, Viscount Baltinglass. Grey sent half of his army under the leadership of one George Moore into County Wicklow to sort out the problem. On August 25th 1580 in a battle known as "The Baltinglass Revolt' O'Byrne defeated the English troops at Glenmalure in County Wicklow (south of Dublin), killing at least 30 of them including Moore himself. He later burned the southern outskirts of Dublin.

O'Byrne was relentlessly pursued by the English who eventually killed him on May 8th 1597. His head was displayed on the battlements of Dublin Castle.

"Black Fitzwilliam" refers to Sir William Fitzwilliam (1526 – 1599), the most experienced Elizabethan administrator in Ireland and reputedly the most corrupt. He presided for a time as Chief Governor of Ireland.

Glen Imaal, Clonmore and Tassagart are towns and townlands which were part of O'Byrne's territories. The "English Pale" was the term used for the region surrounding Dublin on the east coast of Ireland which was a fortified area of English rule in the 16th century. It comprised mainly of the counties of Dublin, Meath, Kildare and Louth.

Carlow is the second smallest county in Ireland (350 square miles) and is adjacent to County Wicklow.

My mother's maiden name is O'Byrne and all of her family come from County Wicklow near the Wicklow/Carlow border.

Which means that I'm probably related in some way or other to Fiach McHugh O'Byrne!

See the swords at Glen Imaal, a-flashing o'er the English Pale
See all the children of the Gael beneath O'Byrne's banners
Rooster of a fighting stock, would you let a Saxon cock
Crow out upon an Irish rock; rise up and teach him manners. *Chorus*

From Tassagart to Clonmore there flows a stream of Saxon gore
And great is Rory Og O'More at sending the loons to Hades
White is sick, Grey has fled; now for Black Fitzwilliam's head
We'll send it over, dripping red, to Queen Liza and her ladies. *Chorus*

~~~~~~~~~~~~~~~

I'm A Rover

(Verses and chorus have the same melody)

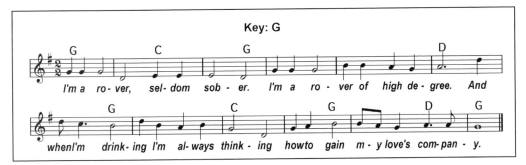

Though the night be dark as dungeon; not a star to be seen above
I will be guided without a stumble into the arms of the one I love.

He stepped up to her bedroom window kneeling gently upon a stone
And he tapped at the bedroom window; "Darling dear, do you lie alone?" *Chorus*

"It's only me dear your own true lover; open up please and let me in
For I have travelled a weary journey and I'm near drenched to my skin".

She opened up with the greatest pleasure; unlocked the door and she let him in
They both embraced and they kissed each other; till the morning they lay as one. *Chorus*

The cocks were waking the birds were whistling; the streams they ran free about the brae
"Remember lass I'm a ploughman's laddie and the farmer I must obey".

"Now my love I must go and leave thee and though the hills they are high above
I will climb them with greater pleasure for I've gained your undying love". *Chorus*

Easy And Slow

The Irish Playwright Sean O'Casey (1880 – 1964) included this ballad in his play "Red Roses For Me", although it is unclear as to whether or not he composed the song himself.
"Red Roses For Me" was written in 1943 and was first performed in the Olympia Theatre, Dublin the same year.
Christchurch, Thomas Street and Kingsbridge are all located in Dublin's south inner city. The Park referred to is the Phoenix Park (see next page)
Dungannon is a town in County Tyrone, Northern Ireland

All along Thomas Street, down to the Liffey; the sunshine was gone and the evening grew dark
Along by Kingsbridge and begod in a jiffy; me arms were around her beyond in the Park.
Chorus

From city or county the girl she's a jewel; and well made for gripping the most of them are
But any young man he is really a fool; if he tries at the first time to go a bit far.
Chorus

Now if you should go to the town of Dungannon; you can search till your eyes they are weary or blind
Be you lying or walking or sitting or running; a lassie like Annie you never will find.
Chorus

68

The Zoological Gardens

This is a bawdy Dublin song about a lusty young couple who decide to 'get up to mischief' in Dublin Zoo.

"Mot" is Dublin slang for girlfriend. "Court" is a quaint Irish verb which means, in its broadest sense, to "get romantically involved with". It would cover every activity from holding hands, to gentle kissing, to a whole lot of other things! I think in this ballad the meaning is "a whole lot of other things!"

Phoenix Park is a beautiful park of about 2000 acres situated in the north-west of Dublin city. The nucleus of the Park was formed by the Duke of Ormond from the confiscated lands of the Knights Hospitallers at Kilmainham. Development of the Park commenced in 1740.

Within the confines of Phoenix Park is Aras an Uachtaráin ('House of the President'). Built in 1751 it was formerly the residence of the British Lord Lieutenant but is now the residence of the President of Ireland.

Dublin Zoo, situated on the north-east side of Phoenix Park, is the second oldest in the world. The Royal Zoological Society was founded in 1830.

The origin of the name "Phoenix Park" is quite amusing. Lord Chesterfield, Viceroy of Ireland when the park was being developed, learned that the fields which were to form part of the park were known in Irish as the "fionn uisge" fields. The fields had been named after a rivulet which used to flow through them. Thinking that the words meant "phoenix" in English, Chesterfield erected a monument in the Park on top of which was placed a phoenix rising from the ashes and thus the name of Phoenix Park was established.

The real meaning of the words "fionn uisge" is "clear stream".

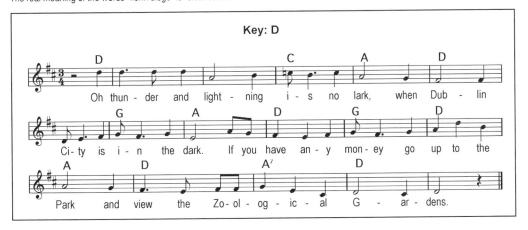

Last Sunday night we had no dough; so I took the mot up to see the Zoo
We saw the lions and kangaroos; inside the Zoological Gardens.

We went up there by Castleknock; said the mot to me "Sure we'll court by the lough"
And I knew she was one of the rare auld stock; inside the Zoological Gardens.

Said the mot to me "My dear friend Jack; would you like a ride on the elephant's back?
If you don't get outta that I'll give you such a crack; inside the Zoological Gardens".

We went up there on our honeymoon; says she to me "If you don't come soon
Sure I'll have to jump in with the hairy baboon; inside the Zoological Gardens".
(Repeat first verse)

Town Of Ballybay

Ballybay is a small town set among low lying hills on the shores of Lough Major - head-water of the Dromore River, a tributary of the River Erne. It is situated in County Monaghan, an inland county in the north-east of the Irish Republic.
Whether or not such a lassie ever existed in Ballybay is best left to the imagination!
"Shimmy" is an old word for night-dress or long vest.
"Courting" is a quaint Irish verb which means, in its broadest sense, to "get romantically involved with". It would cover every activity from holding hands, to gentle kissing, to a whole lot of other things! I think in this ballad (like in "The Zoological Gardens – page 69) the meaning is "a whole lot of other things!"
"Childer" means "children".

She had a wooden leg that was hollow down the middle
She used to tie a string on it and play it like a fiddle
She fiddled in the hall and she fiddled in the alleyway
She didn't give a damn she had to fiddle anyway. *Chorus*

She said she couldn't dance unless she had her wellie on
But when she had it on she could dance as well as anyone
She wouldn't go to bed unless she had her shimmy on
But when she had it on she would go as quick as anyone. *Chorus*

She had lovers by the score, every Tom and Dick and Harry
She was courting night and day but still she wouldn't marry
And then she fell in love with a fella with a stammer
When he tried to run away, she hit him with a hammer. *Chorus*

She had childer up the stairs, she had childer in the brier
Another ten or twelve sitting roaring by the fire
She fed them on potatoes and on soup she made with nettles
And on lumps of hairy bacon that she boiled up in a kettle. *Chorus*

She led a sheltered life, eating porridge and black puddin'
And she terrorised her man till he up'd and died right sudden
And when the husband died she was feeling very sorry
So she rolled him in a bag and she threw him in a quarry. *Chorus*

~~~~~~~~~~~~~~

The Hills Of Kerry

(Verses and chorus have the same melody)

The noble and the brave have departed from our shore
They've gone off to a foreign land where the mighty canyons roar
No more they'll see the shamrock or the hills so dear to me
Or hear the small birds singing all around you, sweet Tralee.
Chorus

No more the sun will shine on that blessed harvest morn
Or hear the reaper singing in the fields of golden corn
There's a balm for every woe and a cure for every pain
But the pretty smile of my darling girl I will never see again.
Chorus

The Sally Gardens

This is a beautiful Irish love song, the lyrics of which were written by William Butler Yeats (1865 – 1939) and published in his collection of poems "Crossways" (1889).
The song is printed in the collection "Irish Country Songs" (1909) edited by Herbert Hughes.
Yeats is regarded as one of the greatest of the Anglo-Irish poets. His mother's family were merchants from County Sligo – hence his many associations with the county. He spent his formative years in London, Dublin and Sligo.
His first works were published in the 1880's and his poetry drew extensively from Gaelic literature and Sligo folklore. Yeats mobilised the nationalist literary groups at the time into a movement for a national artistic revival. This culminated in the foundation of the Irish Literary Theatre, later to be called the Abbey Theatre, in Dublin.
Yeats was awarded the Nobel Prize for Literature in 1923. He served in the Irish Free State as a Senator from 1922 to 1928.
He died in France in 1939 and in 1948 his remains were re-interred in the quiet graveyard in Drumcliffe, County Sligo. The epitaph on his tombstone ("Cast a cold Eye on Life, on Death. Horseman pass by!") has been the subject of many's a lengthy discussion among Irish literary scholars down through the years.
When Yeats was in the town of Ballisodare in County Sligo he heard a local man singing a plaintive folk tune called "The Maids of the Mountain Shore" and this inspired him to write the poem. There was once a row of thatched cottages near the mills at Ballisodare and each of them had a sally garden attached. Yeats considered this to be an ideal place for lovers to meet – hence the song.
Sally (or Salley) comes from the Irish word for willow. Willow rods (osiers) were used in basket-making and for providing scallops for thatching. They were grown specially for those purposes.
County Sligo is situated on the north-east coast of Ireland. County Sligo and parts of adjoining County Leitrim are widely referred to as 'the Yeats Country'.

In a field down by the river my love and I did stand
And on my leaning shoulder she laid her snow-white hand
She bid me take life easy as the grass grows on the weirs
But I was young and foolish and now am full of tears.
(Repeat first verse)

Star Of The County Down

(The chorus melody is the same as the last two lines of the verse)

This ballad was written by Cathal McGarvey (1866 – 1927) to an old Scottish air. The oldest version of the air is in "Tea Table Miscellany", a collection of English and Scottish ballads in three volumes edited by the Scottish poet Allan Ramsay (1686 – 1758). The air has been used for many other ballads, including "Divers And Lazarus", "The Murder Of Maria Martin" and "Claudy Banks".

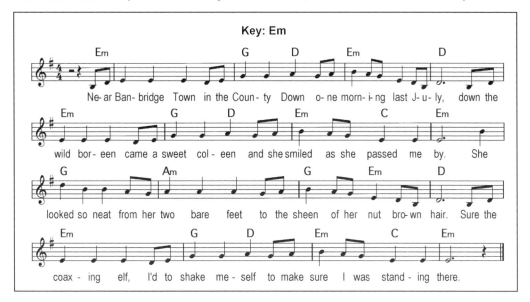

From Bantry Bay up to Derry Quay; from Galway to Dublin Town
No maid I've seen like the sweet colleen that I met in the County Down.

As she onward sped sure I shook my head and I gazed with a feeling quare
And I said, says I, to a passer-by; "whose the maid with the nut-brown hair?"
Oh he smiled at me and with pride says he; "that's the gem of Ireland's crown
She's young Rosie McCann from the banks of the Bann; she's the Star of the County Down".
Chorus

She'd a soft brown eye and a look so sly and a smile like a rose in June
And you craved each note from her lily-white throat as she lilted an Irish tune
At the pattern dance you'd be held in trance as she tripped through a jig or a reel
When her eyes she'd roll she would lift your soul and your heart she would quickly steal.
Chorus

Now I've roamed a bit but was never hit since my travelling days began
But fair and square I surrendered there to the charms of young Rosie McCann
With my heart to let sure no tenant yet did I meet with a shawl or a gown
But in she went and I asked no rent from the Star of the County Down.
Chorus

At the cross-roads fair I'll be surely there and I'll dress in my Sunday clothes
With me shoes all bright and me hat cocked right for a smile from the nut-brown rose
No pipe I'll smoke and no horse I'll yoke let my plough with the rust turn brown
Till a smiling bride by my own fireside be the Star of the County Down.
Chorus

The Wearing Of The Green

There are many versions of this ballad to be found. This version is probably the best known. It was written by Dion Boucicault (1822 – 1890) and included in his play "Arrah-na-Pogue" which was first performed in Dublin in 1865.

Boucicault was born in Dublin, the son of a French refugee and Irish mother. He was a popular playwright in London before the age of twenty. From 1853 to 1869 he moved to the U.S.A. and was equally successful there. He returned to Britain where he died in 1890. Some of his most celebrated works include "The Colleen Bawn", "The Octoroon" and "The Shaugraun".

This is very much a patriotic ballad which laments the suppression by the English administration in Ireland of all Nationalist symbols and sentiment. During the 18th century the colour green became more and more symbolic of Ireland's struggle for freedom. This may be on account of its affiliation to the shamrock, the humble three-leaf plant that had already become a religious emblem and a badge of nationality by 1700. The Cork Volunteers in the 1770's used to sing a song entitled "The Shamrock Cockades". The colour rapidly acquired a political meaning.

The patriot delegates wore green ribands across their shoulders while marching in procession to a convention in Dublin in November 1783. Green handkerchiefs and scarves were waved from the windows as they passed by. When the United Irishmen adopted green as their symbol for a free Ireland the colour was regarded as seditious by the English authorities. In an edition of "The Press" of November 25th 1797 it was written that a green ribbon or handkerchief, even accidentally worn, being regarded as 'an emblem of affection to Ireland' would 'subject a man to imprisonment, transportation, the rope or the bayonet, and expose women to the brutal insults of the common soldiery'.

"Napper Tandy" refers to James Napper Tandy (c. 1737 – 1803), prominent member of the United Irishmen who was involved in the 1798 Rebellion. He was captured in Hamburg, returned to Ireland and sentenced to death but was deported to France in 1803.

This song has, broadly, the same air as "The Rising of the Moon" (page 28) and is also referred to in the ballad "Monto" (page 34)

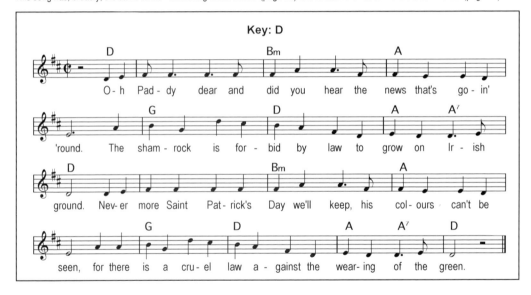

I met with Napper Tandy and he took me by the hand
He said "How's poor old Ireland; please tell how does she stand"
"She is the most distressful land that ever yet was seen
For they're hanging men and women for the wearing of the Green".

And if the colour we must wear is England's cruel red
Let it remind us of the blood that Ireland's sons have shed
Then take the shamrock from your hat and cast it on the sod
And never fear, 'twill take root there though under foot 'tis trod.

When laws can stop the blades of grass from growing where they grow
And when the leaves in summertime their colours dare not show
Then I will change the colour that I wear in my cáibin*
But 'til that day please God I stay a-wearing of the Green.

But if sometime the colour should be torn from Ireland's heart
Her sons with shame and sorrow from our shores will surely part
I've heard a whisper of a land that lies beyond the sea
Where rich and poor stand equal in the light of liberty.

So Erin we must leave you now; cast out by tyrant's hand
We'll treasure mother's blessing from a strange and distant land
Where England's cruel and viscous hand is never to be seen
And where, please God, we'll plough the sod, a-wearing of the Green.

*Pronounced "cawbeen" (cloth cap)

~~~~~~~~~~~~~~

The Leaving Of Liverpool

This is an English emigration ballad which is very popular in Ireland.

I am sailing upon a Yankee sailing ship; Davy Crockett is her name
And her captain's name is Burgess; and they say she is a floating shame.
Chorus

Oh the sun is on the harbour love; and I wish I could remain
For I know it will be a long long time; e'er I see you once again.
Chorus

I Know My Love

This song is printed in the collection "Irish Country Songs" (1909) edited by Herbert Hughes where he states that this is an old song which originated in the west of Ireland. Hughes says that in the counties of Galway and Clare the ballad is usually sung in alternate verses of Irish and English.
A longer version of this ballad is said to exist in Scotland.
Mardyke is an area in Cork City in the south of Ireland and the "hall" referred to in the ballad is probably St. Francis' Hall where many's a good dance or 'hop' took place over the years!

There is a dance house down in Mardyke; 'tis there my true love goes every night
He takes a strange girl upon his knee; and don't you think now that vexes me?
Chorus

If my love knew I could wash and wring; if my love knew I could weave and spin
I'd make a suit of the finest kind; but the want of money leaves me behind.
Chorus

I know my love is an arrant rover; I know my love roams the wide world over
In some foreign town he may chance to tarry; and some foreign maid he will surely marry.
Chorus

The Galway Shawl

(Verses and chorus have the same melody)

A shawl is a type of loose cloak usually worn over the head and shoulders by peasant women throughout Ireland into the early 20th century.

Oranmore is a small rural town to the east of Galway city which lies at the head of Oranmore Bay, a creek of the larger Galway Bay, and is situated at the western extremity of the plain which covers central Ireland between Dublin and Galway city.

Donegal is the most north-westerly county in Ireland.

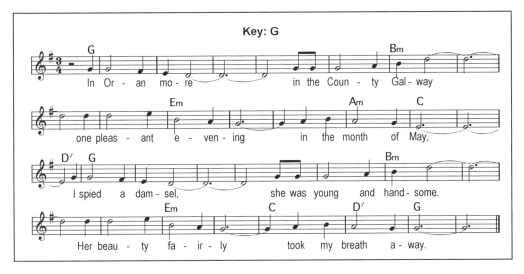

She wore no jewels, no costly diamonds
No paint or powder, no none at all
She wore a bonnet with a ribbon on it
And around her shoulders was a Galway shawl.

As we kept on walking she kept on talking
Till her father's cottage came into view
She said "Come in sir, and meet my father
And for to please him play the Foggy Dew".
Chorus

I played 'The Blackbird' and 'The Stack of Barley'
'Rodney's Glory' and 'The Foggy Dew'
She sang each note like an Irish linnet
And the tears they flowed in her eyes of blue.
Chorus

'Twas early, early, all in the morning
I hit the road for old Donegal
She said "Goodbye sir" and her eyes seemed brighter
And my heart remained with the Galway shawl.
Chorus

77

The Banks Of Claudy

In 1898 a collector of folk songs, Kate Lee, came across a ballad in East Sussex called Claudy Banks in which the lovers were called Betsy and Johnny. Many other similar versions of this song exist where the girl's name changes to Betty, Patsy or Nancy, and the boy's name to William. There is also another ballad called "Claudy Banks" which is quite different to this.

I boldly stepped up to her, I took her by surprise
I own she did not know me, I being dressed in disguise
"Where are you going my fair one, my joy and heart's delight
Where are you going to wander this cold and windy night?"

"It's on the way to Claudy's banks, if you will please to show
Take pity on a stranger, for there I want to go
It's seven long years or better since Johnny has left this shore
He's crossing the wide ocean, where the foaming billows roar".

"He's crossing the wide ocean for honour and for fame
His ship's been wrecked so I've been told down on the Spanish Main"
"It's on the Banks of Claudy fair maiden whereon you stand
Now don't you believe young Johnny, for he's a false young man".

Now when she heard this dreadful news she fell into despair
For the wringing of her tender hands and the tearing of her hair
"If Johnny he be drowned no man alive I'll take
Through lonesome glens and valleys I'll wander for his sake".

Now when he saw her loyalty no longer could he stand
He fell into her arms saying "Betsy I'm the man".
Saying "Betsy I'm the young man who caused you all the pain,
And since we've met on Claudy's banks we'll never part again".

Quare Bungle Rye

The original ballad from which the present one derives was called "The Oyster Girl" and a version is to be found in the Bodleian Library at Oxford University dating back to the 1820's.
Variants of this ballad have been found in Aberdeenshire, Somerset, Northern Ireland and North Carolina under such titles as "The Basket of Oysters", "Eggs In Her Basket" and "Quare Bungo Rye".

Thought Jack to himself now what can this be
But the finest of whiskey from old Germany
Smuggled up in a basket and sold on the sly
And the name that it goes by is quare bungle rye roddy rye.
Chorus

Jack gave her a pound and he thought nothing strange
She said "hold the basket till I run for your change"
Jack looked in the basket and a baby did spy
"Begorra" says he "This is quare bungle rye roddy rye!".
Chorus

Now to get the child christened was Jack's first intent
And to get the child christened to the parson he went
Said the parson to Jack, "What will he go by?"
"Bedad now", says Jack, "call him quare bungle rye roddy rye".
Chorus

Now all you bold sailors who roam on the town
Beware of the damsels who skip up and down
Take a look in their baskets as they pass you by
Or else they may sell you some quare bungle rye roddy rye.
Chorus

The Mermaid

This ballad dates back to at least the mid 1700's and was also known as 'Waves On The Sea' and 'The Wrecked Ship'. It appeared in the Francis Child collection of ballads 'The English and Scottish Popular Ballads', a five volume work published between 1882 and 1898.
There was widespread superstition among sailors that the sighting of a mermaid was an omen of shipwreck.

Then up spoke the captain of our gallant ship and a fine old man was he
"This fishy mermaid has warned me of our doom. We will sink to the bottom of the sea".
Chorus

Then up spoke the mate of our gallant ship and a fine spoken man was he
Saying "I have a wife in Brooklyn by the sea and tonight a widow she will be".
Chorus

Then up spoke the cabin-boy of our gallant ship and a brave young lad was he
"I have a sweetheart in Salem by the sea and tonight she'll be weeping for me".
Chorus

Then up spoke the cook of our gallant ship and a crazy old butcher was he
"I care so much more for my skillets and my pans than I do for the bottom of the sea".
Chorus

Then three times around spun our gallant ship and three times around spun she
Three times around spun our gallant ship and she sank to the bottom of the sea.
Chorus

Sean South From Garryowen

From about 1956 to 1963 the Irish Republican Army in the Republic of Ireland waged a 'border campaign' on police barracks and Custom Posts around the borders between Northern Ireland and the Republic.

This song is an Irish patriotic ballad commemorating a failed attack on a Royal Ulster Constabulary barracks in Brookborough, County Fermanagh on New Year's Eve 1957. The small band of men, members of the Patrick Pearse Column of the I.R.A., were led by Sean South who as the ballad says came from Garryowen, a district of Limerick city.

The raid went disastrously wrong and Sean South along with Feargal O'Hanlon from County Monaghan were killed in the ensuing skirmish.

Sean South's funeral was held on January 5th 1958 and the massive cortege included public representative and members of the Irish Government. He was buried in the Republican Plot in Mount St. Laurence Cemetary, Limerick.

Dublin, Cork, Fermanagh, Tyrone and Limerick are all counties in Ireland.

The reference to "Shannon" is the River Shannon, the largest river in Ireland. It flows out to the sea through Limerick city.

"Plunkett" is Joseph Plunkett (1887 – 1916), one of the leaders of the 1916 Rising and a signatory of the Irish Proclamation.

"Pearse" is Padraig Pearse (1879 – 1916), the leader of the 1916 Rising and also a signatory of the Irish Proclamation.

"Tone" is Theobald Wolfe Tone (1763 – 1798), one of the chief instigators of the 1798 Rebellion.

And as they moved along the street up to the barracks door
They scorned the dangers they would meet; the fate that lay in store
They were fighting for old Ireland's cause to claim their very own
And their leader was a Limerick man, Sean South from Garryowen.

But the sergeant spied their daring plan, he spied them through the door
With their sten guns and their rifle shots a hail of death did roar
And when that awful night had passed two men lay cold as stone
And one was from a border town and one from Garryowen.

No more he'll hear the seagulls cry o'er the murmuring Shannon tide
For he fell beneath a northern sky, brave Hanlon by his side
He has gone to join that gallant band of Plunkett, Pearce and Tone
Another martyr for old Ireland, Sean South from Garryowen.

The Black Velvet Band

(Verses and chorus have the same melody)

It is thought that this old ballad may have originated in Belfast. Some versions of the song begin with the lines "In a neat little town they call Belfast".
The first known printed version was contained in "Folk Songs From Hampshire" (1909) edited by George Gardiner.
This very popular Irish ballad carries with it a stern warning about never trusting the fairer sex!
Many Irish men and women were deported, or 'transported' to Van Diemen's Land (originally referring to Tasmania, but the name was later used colloquially to refer to Australia itself) by the British authorities during the 19th century - often for very petty crimes.
Tasmanian whalers also have a song similar to this one called "The Hat With The Velvet Band".
"Kilkenny" city is in central Ireland, and is the capital of County Kilkenny.

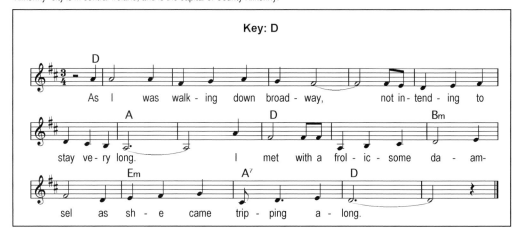

A gold watch she took out of her pocket and placed it right into my hand
On the very first time that I saw her; bad luck to the black velvet band.

Her eyes they shone like diamonds; you'd think she was queen of the land
With her hair thrown over her shoulder; tied up with a black velvet band.

'Twas in the town of Kilkenny; an apprentice to trade I was bound
With gaiety and bright amusement to see all the days go around
Till misfortune and trouble came over me which forced me to stray from the land
Far away from my friends and relations; betrayed by the black velvet band.
Chorus

Before judge and jury next morning the both of us did appear
A gentleman swore to his jewellery and the case against us was clear
Seven long years' transportation away down to Van Diemen's Land
Far away from my friends and relations to follow the black velvet band.
Chorus

Now all you brave young Irish lads a warning please gather from me
Beware of the pretty young damsels you meet all around Kilkenny
They'll treat you with whiskey and porter until you're unable to stand
And before you have time for to leave them you'll be sent down to Van Diemen's Land.
Chorus

Let Him Go, Let Him Tarry

(Verses and chorus have the same melody)

"Courting" is a quaint Irish verb which means, in its broadest sense, to "get romantically involved with". It would cover every activity from holding hands, to gentle kissing, to a whole lot of other things!

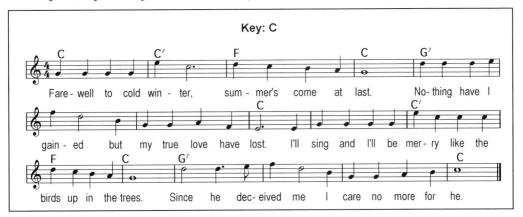

Let him go, let him tarry, let him sink or let him swim
He doesn't care for me nor I don't care for him
He can go and get another that I hope he will enjoy
For I'm going to marry a far nicer boy.

He wrote me a letter saying he was very bad
I sent him back an answer saying I was awful glad
He wrote me another saying he was well and strong
But I care no more for him than the ground he walks upon.
Chorus

Some of his friends they have a good kind wish for me
Others of his friends sure they could hang me on a tree
But soon I'll let them see my love and soon I'll let them know
That I can get a new sweetheart at any place I go.
Chorus

He can go to his old mother now and set her mind at ease
I hear she's an old woman and very hard to please
It's slighting me and talking ill is what she's always done
Because I was courting her great big ugly son.
Chorus

The Golden Jubilee

(Verses and chorus have the same melody)

Tralee is the principal town of County Kerry and the gateway to the Dingle Peninsula, situated in the south-west of Ireland. There's another ballad in this book about a girl from Tralee. See "The Rose of Tralee" – page 16.

Put on your old knee britches and your coat of emerald green
Take off that hat me darling Pat, put on your old cáibín*
For today's our Golden Wedding and I'll have you all to know
Just how we looked when we were wed fifty years ago

Oh well do I remember how we danced on the village green
You held me in your arms dear Pat and called me your colleen
Your hair was like a raven's wing but now it's turning grey
Come over here my sweetheart dear and hear what I've to say.
Chorus

Oh well do I remember when first I was your bride
In the little chapel on the hill where we stood side by side
Of good friends we've had plenty, of troubles we've had few
Come over here my sweetheart dear and here's what you must do.
Chorus

*Pronounced "cawbeen" (cloth cap)

Three Lovely Lassies From Kimmage

This is a great old ballad, very popular in Dublin, and it's also very easy to sing!
Kimmage is a district of south Dublin city and this ballad tells the story of a couple who get married and have no choice but to move in with their parents until the Local Authorities provide them with a house of their own at nominal rent under the Public Housing Scheme. A position on the waiting list was determined by a points system and the more children the couple had, the more points they would receive and the quicker they would be given their own house. Hence the sentiments echoed in the last verse.

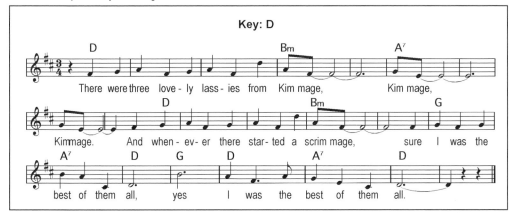

Well the cause of the row is Joe Cashin, Joe Cashin, Joe Cashin
For he told me he thought I looked smashin'
At the dance at the Adelaide Hall; at the dance at the Adelaide Hall.

He told me he thought we should marry, should marry, should marry
For he said it was foolish to tarry
So he lent me the price of the ring; so he lent me the price of the ring.

When he has a few jars he goes frantic, goes frantic, goes frantic
But he's tall and he's dark and romantic
And I love him in spite of it all; and I love him in spite of it all.

Well me dad said he'd give us a present, a present, a present
A picture of a lovely pheasant
The picture will hang on the wall; yes the picture will hang on the wall.

I went to the Tenancy Section, the Section, the Section
The T.D.* before the election
Said he'd get me a house near me ma; said he's get me a house near me ma.

Well I'll get a house the man said it, said it, said it
When I've five or six kids to me credit
In the meantime we'll live with me ma; in the meantime we'll live with me ma.

*Irish member of Parliament

Maids When You're Young

(Verses and chorus have the same melody)

This bawdy ballad is well known in Ireland, England, Scotland and North America. It first appeared in 1870 in a collection of ballads by David Herd and the song was entitled "Scant Of Love, Want Of Love"

"Courting" is a quaint Irish verb which means, in its broadest sense, to "get romantically involved with". It would cover every activity from holding hands, to gentle kissing, to a whole lot of other things! I think that the girl in this ballad wants it to mean "a whole lot of other things!"

For he's got no folurum fol diddle-i-urum da
He's got no folurum fol diddle-i-aye
He's got no flurum, he's lost his ding-durum da
Maids when you're young never wed an auld man.

When we went to church, hey ding-durum da
When we went to church me being young
When we went to church he left me in the lurch
Maids when you're young never wed an auld man. *Chorus*

When we went to bed, hey ding-durum da
When we went to bed me being young
When we went to bed he lay like he was dead
Maids when you're young never wed an auld man. *Chorus*

I threw my leg over him hey ding-durum da
I threw my leg over him me being young
I threw my leg over him, damn nearly smothered him
Maids when you're young never wed an auld man. *Chorus*

When he went to sleep, hey ding-durum da
When he went to sleep me being young
When he went to sleep out of bed I did creep
Into the arms of a willing young man
Chorus change:- "And I found his falurum, fol diddle-i-urum da", etc.

The Boys Of Fairhill

A very popular ballad in Cork city and almost as well known as "The Banks" (page 31). Fairhill is a suburb of north Cork and this ballad is in praise of the local hurling team.

Hurling is one of our two most popular national games in Ireland (Gaelic Football being the other). There is a great devotion to hurling in Cork and there have been many fine Cork hurling teams victorious in the All Ireland Hurling Championships.

"Crubeens" are boiled pig's feet, a very popular dish in Cork. Patrick's Bridge is the main bridge over the River Lee which flows through Cork city and there is a statue of Father Matthew located beside the bridge. Father Matthew, known as the Apostle of Temperance, dedicated most of his life to persuading Irishmen to give up 'the demon drink'.

We'll go down by Sunday's Well, what might happen, who can tell
Heads, they might roll or some blood it might spill
We'll come back by Blackpool way when we've overcome the fray
"Here's up them all!" says the Boys of Fairhill.

Jimmy Barry hooks the ball, we'll hook Jimmy, ball and all
"Here's up them all!" says the Boys of Fairhill
The Rockies thought they were the stars till they met the Saint Finbarr's
"Here's up them all!" says the Boys of Fairhill.

Kathy Barry sells crubeens, fairly bursting at the seams
Sure for to cure and more sure for to kill
The stench on Patrick's Bridge is wicked, how does Father Matthew stick it
"Here's up them all!" says the Boys of Fairhill.

The Waxie's Dargle

The air of this popular Dublin ballad is a well known and recognised melody entitled "The Girl I left Behind Me" and was first published in Dublin in 1791. A traditional fife tune, it was a very popular patriotic song during the American Revolution.

In Dublin, the 'Waxies' were the people who waxed bootlaces. The term was also used for candlemakers. In any event, they were without doubt members of the 'working classes' on the lower rungs of the social ladder in Dublin.

At the turn of the century in Dublin it was the practice for well-to-do folk to take summer breaks in the fashionable seaside town of Bray in County Wicklow, about 20 miles south of Dublin city. Bray was a very popular town for wealthy Dubliners and a river ran near the town called the Dargle.

Once every year the Waxies held an annual outing. They couldn't afford to go all the way the Bray so they used to go to Sandymount Strand, an extensive beach on the south side of Dublin. Sandymount Strand became known as 'The Waxie's Dargle' as it was their equivalent of the fashionable seaside resort of Bray.

In this ballad, two Dublin women are contemplating a visit to the 'Waxie's Dargle' but don't have the necessary money.

"Monto Town" is a reference to the red-light district around Montgomery Street in the heart of Dublin. See "Monto" - page 34.

"Galway Races" is an annual racing festival held in Galway each year. See "The Galway Races" - page 36.

"Capel Street" is a Dublin street on the north side of the River Liffey renowned for its pawnbroking shops. In the second verse of the ballad one of the women hopes to pawn her husband's trouser braces and travel to the Galway races with the proceeds.

In some versions of the ballad 'young Kill McArdle' is replaced by 'Uncle McArdle'.

Says my oul' one to your oul' one "Will ye come to the Galway Races?"
Says your oul' one to my oul' one "With the price of me oul' lad's braces
I went down to Capel Street to the Jewman moneylender
But they wouldn't give me a couple of bob for me oul' lad's new suspenders". *Chorus*

Says my oul' one to your oul' one "We have no beef or mutton"
But if we go down to Monto town we might get a drink for nothin'
Here's a piece of advice for you which I got from an oul' fishmonger
When food is scarce and you see the hearse you'll know you died of hunger". *Chorus*

The Snowy-Breasted Pearl

The lyrics of this ballad were translated from Irish by George Petrie and appear along with the air (in 4/4 timing) in his "Ancient Music of Ireland" (1855). The title of the ballad in Petrie's book is "The Pearl Of The White Breast". Petrie acknowledges that he obtained the words and music from a Mr. Eugene Curry of County Clare who was of the opinion that the song did not originate in County Clare but rather somewhere else on the west coast of Ireland. Petrie confesses, however, that in his own musical research in the west of Ireland he had never come across the air.

There is also an air and some lyrics which appear in "A General Collection of Ancient Irish Music" by Edward Bunting (1796) under the title "The Pearl Of The White Breast" but neither the melody nor lyrics relate to this version of the song.

A great version of this ballad was recorded some time ago by the Irish folk group, The Wolfe Tones.

Oh thou blooming milk-white dove to whom I have aimed my love
Do not ever thus reprove my constancy
There are maidens would be mine with a wealth in land and kine
If my heart would but incline to turn from thee
But a kiss with welcome bland, and touch of thy fair hand
Are all that I'd demand, would'st thou not spurn
For if not mine dear girl
Oh, snowy-breasted pearl
May I never from the fair with life return.

Slievenamon

This ballad is recognised by Tipperary folk throughout the world as their County Anthem and can be heard loud and clear at all major 'Tipp' occasions, particularly Hurling and Gaelic Football matches.

It was written by Charles J. Kickham (1828 – 1882) and was originally known as "The Maid Of Slievenamon". Kickham came from Mullinahone in County Tipperary (situated in central Ireland) and was a member of a prosperous family. He was a journalist and nationalist and joined the Fenian movement in 1861.

Two years later he moved to Dublin and worked on the Fenian weekly newspaper 'The Irish People'. He was arrested and imprisoned in 1865 and released in 1869. By this time he was regarded as one of the leading nationalists in Ireland. In 1873 he was appointed President of the revolutionary Irish Republican Brotherhood (an organisation which evolved out of the failed 1867 Fenian Rising), a position he held until his death in 1882.

He was a noted ballad writer and also wrote a number of books, of which "Knocknagow" is his most famous.

The mountains of Slievenamon are located in the south-east of County Tipperary. The heatherlands, meadows and woods of Slievenamon cover an area of about 7,000 acres. The Slievenamon mountains rise to 2,370 feet at their highest point and dominate the surrounding plains.

There is another Irish ballad called "Sliabh Na mBan", a nationalist ballad about the plight of Ireland following another defeat in her fight for freedom.

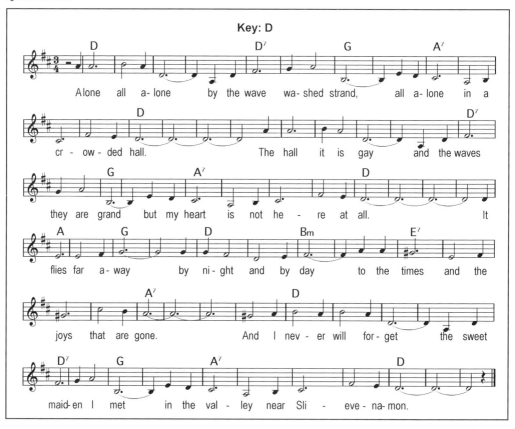

Twas not the grace of her queenly air; nor her cheek of the rose's glow
Nor her soft dark eyes or her flowing hair; nor was it her lily-white brow
'Twas the soul of truth and of melting youth and a smile like the summer's dawn
That stole my heart away on that soft summer day in the valley near Slievenamon.

In the Festival Hall by the wave-washed shore, there my restless spirit cries
"My love, oh my love, shall I ne'er see you more and my land will you never uprise?"
By night and by day, I ever ever pray while so lonely my life flows on
But to see our flag unrolled and my true-love to enfold in the valley near Slievenamon.

The Spanish Lady

This is one of my favourite ballads in the book but unfortunately I have no knowledge of its history.
Stoneybatter is a district situated on Dublin's northside. Patrick's Close and the Gloucester Diamond are areas located in Dublin city centre.
"Napper Tandy" refers to James Napper Tandy (c. 1737 – 1803) who was a prominent member of the United Irishmen and was involved in the 1798 Rising. He lived in Dublin city centre. He was captured in Hamburg, returned to Ireland and sentenced to death, but was deported to France in 1803.

As I came back through Dublin city at the hour of half past eight
Who should I spy but the Spanish Lady brushing her hair in the broad daylight
First she tossed it then she brushed it; on her lap was a silver comb
In all my life I ne'er did see a maid so fair since I did roam.
Chorus

As I went back through Dublin city as the sun began to set
Who should I spy but the Spanish Lady catching a moth in a golden net
When she saw me then she fled me, lifting her petticoat over her knee
In all my life I ne'er did see a maid so shy as the Spanish Lady.
Chorus

I wandered north and I wandered south through Stoneybatter and Patrick's Close
Up and around by the Gloucester Diamond and back by Napper Tandy's house
Old age has laid her hand upon me, cold as a fire of ashy coals
In all my life I ne'er did see a maid so sweet as the Spanish Lady.
Chorus

Highland Paddy

This is a patriotic ballad made famous through recordings of it by many Irish folk and ballad groups.
Kilkenny city is a large town situated in central Ireland, with its civic and ecclesiastical roots deep in the past.
The Fenians were a group of revolutionary Irish patriots. The movement originated in the USA but eventually spread to Ireland following the collapse of the Young Ireland movement of the 1840's.
The Fenians attempted a rebellion in 1867 but they were easily and swiftly defeated by the British administration.
'Fenian' became synonymous with 'rebel' in the language of the loyalists and is still used to this day in that context.

And in the morning we rose early, just before the break of dawn
Blackbirds singing in the bushes, greetings to a smiling morn
Gather 'round me men of Ireland, all ye Fenians gather round
Hand to hand with sword and musket, spill the blood upon this holy ground.
Chorus

There is a glen beside the river, just outside Kilkenny town
There we met this noble captain, men lay dying upon the ground
There is a grave down by the river, a mile outside Kilkenny town
There we laid our noble Captain, birds were silent when this Fenian died.
Chorus

For all my life I will remember, I'll remember night and day
That once I rode into Kilkenny and I heard the noble Captain say.
Chorus

Paddy's Green Shamrock Shore

Key: C

Oh fa - re thee well sweet I - re - la - n - d my o - wn dear na - tive home. It brea - ks my heart, t - o se - e friends part for it's then that the tear- drops will fall. I'm o - n my way to A - m - er - ic - ay will I e'er see my home land once more. For n - ow I leave my o - wn true lo - ve on Pad - dy's green sham - rock shore.

Our ship she lies at anchor now; she's standing by the quay
May fortune bright shine down each night as we sail all across the sea
Many ships have been lost, many lives it has cost on the journey that lies before
With a tear in my eye I'm bidding goodbye to Paddy's green shamrock shore.

From Londonderry we did set sail; it being the fourth of May
On a sturdy ship to cover the trip across to Americay
Fresh water then did we take in; one hundred barrels or more
For fear we'd be short before reaching port far from the shamrock shore.

Two of our anchors we did weigh before we left the quay
All down the river we were towed till we came to the open sea
We saw that night the grandest sight we ever saw before
The sun going down 'tween sea and sky far from Paddy's green shamrock shore.

Early next morn, sea-sick and forlorn, not one of us was free
And I myself was confined to bed with no one to pity me
No father or mother or sister or brother to raise my head when sore
That made me think of the family I left back on Paddy's green shamrock shore.

So fare thee well my own true love I think of you night and day
A place in my mind you surely will find although I'm so far away
Though I am alone and away from my home I'll think of the good time before
Until the day I can make my way back to Paddy's green shamrock shore.

Muirsheen Durkin

(Verses and chorus have the same melody)

This is an emigration ballad written to the melody of the Irish air "Cailiní Deas Mhuigheo" (The Beautiful Girls of Mayo"), though presented in a somewhat light-hearted manner. Instead of bemoaning the fact that he has to leave Ireland the singer is quite looking forward to making his fortune in "far Americay". Indeed, many Irish emigrants did just that over the centuries!

It is estimated that at least 8 million Irish men and women emigrated from Ireland between 1801 and 1921 and many more left during the depression years of the 20th century. The statement therefore by President Mary Robinson in December 1990, that there are at least 70 million people throughout the world who claim to be of Irish descent, is not an exaggeration.

The most common destination for Irish emigrants prior to the 1860's was Canada; between then and the First World War it was the U.S.A., and from then on it was Great Britain.

"Courting" is a quaint Irish term which means, in its broadest sense, to "get romantically involved with". It would cover every activity from holding hands, to gentle kissing, to a whole lot of other things!

Obviously the singer in this ballad spent some time the south of Ireland, as the towns of Blarney, Kanturk, Killarney, Passage and Cobh (formerly Queenstown) are all located in the counties of Cork and Kerry. It looks as if he was a busy man down there!

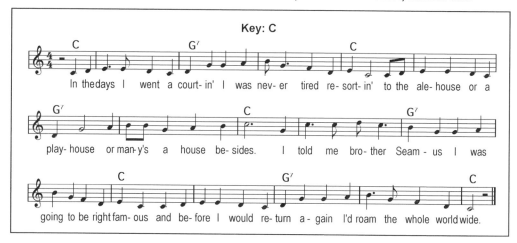

Goodbye Muirsheen Durkin, sure I'm sick and tired of workin'
No more I'll dig the praties, no longer I'll be fooled
For sure's me name is Carney I'll be off to Californee
And instead of digging praties I'll be digging lumps of gold.

I've courted girls in Blarney, in Kanturk and in Killarney
In Passage and in Queenstown; that is the Cobh of Cork
But goodbye to all this pleasure sure I'm off to seek me leisure
And the next time you will hear from me is a letter from New York.
Chorus

So goodbye all ye boys at home I'm sailing far across the foam
I'm going to make me fortune in far Americay
There's gold and money plenty for the poor and for the gentry
And when I do return again I never more will stray.
Chorus

Roddy McCorley

This ballad was written by Anna Johnston (1866 – 1902) under the pseudonym 'Ethna Carbury'. She was born in Ballymena in County Antrim. She was the editor of the Belfast Republican journal "The Sean Van Vocht" ("The Poor Old Woman") with Alice Milligan.

She married the folklorist and storyteller Seamus McManus from Mountcharles in County Donegal in 1902. Her poetry and that of her husband was published in a volume called "We Sang for Ireland" (1902).

This ballad has the same air as "Sean South from Garryowen" (page 81) and is dedicated to the memory of Roddy McCorley, a patriot who took part in the 1798 Rebellion in County Antrim. McCorley was a Presbyterian from Duneane. He was on the run for over a year after the Rebellion but was betrayed and was hanged in the town of Toome Bridge in County Antrim (Northern Ireland) on February 28th, 1800. It is said that his body was buried directly beneath the gallows.

Ironically, Toome Bridge derives its name from the Irish word 'Tuaim' meaning 'burial mound'.

For further information about the 1798 Rebellion see the Additional Notes at the front of this book.

When he last stepped up that street, his shining pike in hand
Behind him marched in grim array a stalwart earnest band
For Antrim town, for Antrim town he led them to the fray
And young Roddy McCorley goes to die on the bridge of Toome today.

Up the narrow streets he boldly steps, smiling, proud and young
Around the hemp rope on his neck his golden ringlets clung
There was never a tear in his blue eyes, both sad and bright are they
For young Roddy McCorley goes to die on the bridge of Toome today

There was never a one of all our dead more bravely fell in fray
Than he who marches to his fate on the bridge of Toome today
True to the last as we say goodbye he treads the upward way
And young Roddy McCorley goes to die on the bridge of Toome today.

Kelly From Killane

This ballad was written by P.J. McCall who also wrote "Boulavogue" (page 126).
The song honours John Kelly, one of the local heroes of the 1798 Rebellion in Wexford.
Kelly was the son of a Killane merchant and took part in the Battle of New Ross. He was under orders from Bagenal Harvey, the Wexford commander, to proceed with an army of 800 United Irishmen towards New Ross and to attack the English outposts but under no circumstances to attack the town itself. Harvey had worked out a detailed plan to take New Ross by simultaneously attacking through its three main gates. But on June 5th 1798, for reasons which are to this day unknown, Kelly's forces attacked New Ross through the 'Three Bullet Gate', successfully broke through, and continued on into the town itself. The ensuing disarray, confusion and lack of direction eventually led to the defeat of the rebel forces.
Kelly was wounded in Michael Street, New Ross and was recovering in Wexford Town when he was arrested by the English. He was subsequently hanged on Wexford Bridge.
'Shelmalier' is a townland of Wexford and the farmers there were accustomed to hunting wild fowl on the North Sloblands. Their 'long barrelled guns' proved to be very effective against the English forces during the rebellion. 'Forth' and 'Bargy' are also townlands in County Wexford.
For further information on the 1798 Rebellion see the Additional Notes at the front of this book.

"Tell me who is that giant with the gold curling hair; he who rides at the head of your band
Seven feet is his height with some inches to spare; and he looks like a king in command"
"Ah my lads, that's the pride of the bold Shelmaliers; 'mongst our greatest of heroes, a man
Fling your beavers aloft and give three ringing cheers; for John Kelly, the boy from Killane".

Enniscorthy's in flames and old Wexford is won; and the Barrow, tomorrow, we will cross
On a hill o'er the town we have planted a gun; that will batter the gateway of Ross
All the Forth men and Bargy men march o'er the heath; with brave Harvey to lead on the van
But the foremost of all in that grim gap of death; will be Kelly, the boy from Killane.

But the gold sun of freedom grew darkened at Ross; and it set by the Slaney's red waves
And poor Wexford, stripped naked, hung high on a cross; and her heart pierced by traitors and slaves
Glory O! Glory O! To her brave sons who died; for the cause of long downtrodden man
Glory O! To Mount Leinster's own darling and pride; dauntless Kelly, the boy from Killane.

~~~~~~~~~~~~

The German Clockwinder

(Verses and chorus have the same melody)

This ballad, full of innuendo and double-meaning, is a derivative of an old English Ballad called "The German Musicianer" in which the gentleman in question tuned the woman's piano as opposed to winding her clock.
It doesn't really matter – it all came down to the same thing in the end!

With me toor-a-lumma-lumma, toor-a-lumma-lumma, toor-a-lie-ay
Toor-a-lie, oor-a-lie, orr-a-lie-ay
Toor-a-lumma-lumma, toor-a-lumma-lumma, toor-a-lie-ay
Toor-a-lie, oor-a-lie, orr-a-lie-ay.

Now there was a young lady from Grosvenor Square; who said that her clock was in need of repair
In walks the bold German and to her delight; in less than five minutes he had her put right.
Chorus

Now as they were seated down on the floor; there started a very loud knock on the door
In walked her husband and great was his shock; to see the bold German wind up his wife's clock.
Chorus

The husband says he "Oh wife, Mary Ann; don't let that bold German come in here again
He wound up your clock and left mine on the shelf; if your oul' clock needs winding I'll wind it myself!"
Chorus

A Nation Once Again

This ballad has been one of the main anthems of Irish revolutionary movements for the past 150 years.
Written by Thomas Davis (1814 – 1845), the ballad reflects the aspiration of the Young Ireland movement of the 1840's of which he was leader. Davis, the son of an English army surgeon, was born in County Cork. Educated at Trinity College in Dublin, he espoused many of his thoughts and ideas for Irish Nationhood in 'The Nation' a weekly newspaper which he founded in October 1842. He also sought to bring a sense of 'Irish Nationality' to the Irish people through the ballads published in 'The Nation', this being one of them. He also wrote another ballad in this book, "The West's Awake" (page 138).
Davis sought to introduce a new concept to the writing of Irish 'national' ballads. Prior to 'The Nation' most ballads were written as spontaneous and emotional reactions to events and circumstances as they occurred. Davis was determined to utilise the Irish ballad as an instrument to enable and encourage Irish people to reflect on the principle of Irish nationhood. In 'The Nation' of 11th March 1843 he wrote "We furnish political songs to stimulate flagging zeal, or create it where it does not exist". In the second edition of the paper (22nd October 1842) it stated, "We will endeavour to teach the people to sing the songs of their country that may keep alive in their minds the love of fatherland".
'The Nation' was suppressed by the British administration in 1848 and was revived again by a colleague of Davis, Charles Gavan Duffy, in 1849. It continued until 1897.
Davis died suddenly in September 1845 from an attack of scarlet fever at the age of 31 years.

And from that time through wildest woe that hope has shone a far light
Nor could love's brightest summer glow, outshine that solemn starlight
It seemed to watch above my head in forum field and fane
Its angel voice sang 'round my head, a nation once again. *Chorus*

It whispered too that freedom's ark and service high and holy
Would be profaned by feelings dark and passions vain or lowly
For freedom comes from God's right hand and needs a godly train
And righteous men must make our land a nation once again. *Chorus*

So as I grew from boy to man I bent me to that bidding
My spirit of each selfish plan and cruel passion ridding
For thus I hoped some day to aid; oh can such hope be vain
When my dear country can be made a nation once again. *Chorus*

The Moonshiner

(Verses and chorus have the same melody)

This pleasant ballad is about that most popular of Irish alcoholic beverages, 'Poitín' or 'Poteen'. - also the subject of the ballad "Let the Grasses Grow" (page 30). There are many other ballads dedicated to the pastime of making and drinking this illicit libation and of avoiding the local constabulary and excise men in the process. All the ballads I know are in praise of this activity!

Because of the high taxation imposed on alcohol many's an Irish person has been reduced to the illicit distillation of their own alcoholic drinks. Some of them made quite a business out of it and managed by all sorts of means to stay one step ahead of the Law. Poitín is a colourless liquid distilled using grain, normally barley. The practice of making poitín expanded rapidly following the Revenue Act of 1779. This Act of Parliament banned small stills and imposed heavy duties on others. Poitín was not only a cheap source of alcohol but it was often of much better quality than the official 'parliament whiskey'.

A Peace Preservation Force was established by the British Prime Minister, Robert Peel in 1814 to deal with widespread rural unrest throughout Ireland. Under the command of a Stipendiary Magistrate these first 'peelers' could be quickly deployed to any area which had been proclaimed as 'disturbed'. One of the first deployments of this new force was not in relation to rural unrest or disturbance, but was against illegal distillers in Inishowen Co. Donegal in 1817.

The practice began to decline from 1857 onwards when the Royal Irish Constabulary assumed responsibility (taking over from the ineffectual Revenue Police) for the detection of illicit stills and the prosecution of the poitín makers.

Poitín was particularly popular in rural areas and the ballad mentions Galway, a county on the West coast of Ireland. Rumour has it that poitín was (and probably still is!) extensively distilled in the Galway area.

The counties of Donegal, Sligo and Leitrim are also on the west and north-west coasts of Ireland.

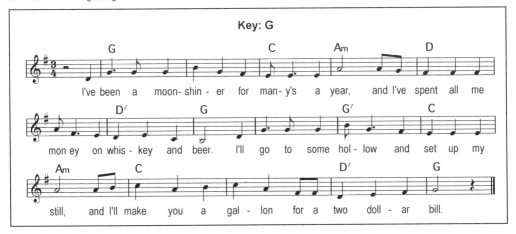

I'm a rambler, I'm a gambler, I'm a long way from home
And if you don't like me then leave me alone
I'll eat when I'm hungry, I'll drink when I'm dry
And if the moonshine don't kill me I'll live till I die.

I'll go to some hollow in this country
Ten gallons of wash and I'll go on a spree
No woman to follow and the world is all mine
I love none so well as I love the moonshine. *Chorus*

Moonshine, dear moonshine, oh how I love thee
You killed my poor father but dare you try me
Bless all the moonshiners and bless the moonshine
Its breath smells as sweet as the dew on the vine. *Chorus*

There's moonshine for Molly and moonshine for May
Moonshine for Tom and he'll sing all the day
Moonshine for me breakfast, moonshine for me tea
Moonshine oh me hearties! It's moonshine for me! *Chorus*

Mush Mush

(Verses and chorus have the same melody)

This is an old ballad popular throughout Ireland. The ballad seems to start in the middle of a story and there are obviously some verses before the first one here, but I have never come across them.

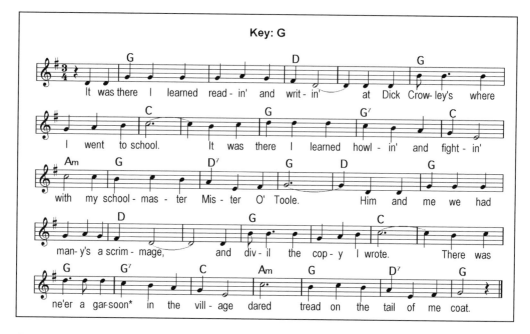

Singing mush mush mush toor-a-lie-addy; sing mush mush mush toor-a-lie-ay
There was ne'er a gassoon* in the village dared tread on the tail of me coat.

'Twas there I learned all of my courting; many lessons I took in the art
Till Cupid the blackguard, in sporting; an arrow drove straight through my heart
Molly Connor she lived right beside me; and tender lines to her I wrote
If you dare say one wrong word against her; I'll tread on the tail of your coat.
Chorus

But a blackguard called Mickey Moloney; he stole her affections away
He had money and I hadn't any; so I sent him a challenge next day
That evening we met at the woodbine; the Shannon we crossed in a boat
And I leathered him with my shillelagh; for he trod on the tail of my coat.
Chorus

My fame spread abroad through the nation; and folks came a-flocking to see
And they cried out without hesitation; "You're a fighting man, Billy McGee"
I cleaned out the Finnegan faction; and I licked all the Murphys afloat
If you're in for a row or a ruction just tread on the tail of me coat.
Chorus

* Young boy

Reilly's Daughter

Key: G

As I was sit-ting by the fire, eat-ing spuds and drink-ing por-ter, sud-den-ly a thought came in-to my mind: I think I'll mar-ry old Reil-ly's daugh-ter! *Gid-dy-i-ay, gid-dy-i-ay, gid-dy-i-ay for the one eyed Reil-ly, gid-dy-i-ay. (BoomBoom Boom). Bang it on your old bass drum!*

For Reilly played on the big bass drum
Reilly had a mind for murder and slaughter
Reilly had one big red glittering eye
And he kept that eye on his lovely daughter.
Chorus

Her hair was black and her eyes were blue
The colonel and the major and the captain sought her
The sergeant and the private and the drummer boy too
But they never had a chance with aul' Reilly's daughter.
Chorus

I got me a ring and a parson too
I got me a scratch in the married quarter
Settled me down to a peaceful life
As happy as a king with Reilly's daughter.
Chorus

I hear a sudden footstep on the stair
It's the one-eyed Reilly and he lookin' for slaughter
With two pistols in his hand
Searching for the man who had married his daughter.
Chorus

I took auld Reilly by the hair
Rammed his head into a bucket of water
Fired his pistols in the air
A damned sight quicker than I married his daughter.
Chorus

The Cliffs Of Doneen

The Cliffs of Doneen are situated on the west coast of Ireland between the towns of Ballybunion and Ballylongford (County Kerry) on the estuary of the River Shannon with fine views across to County Clare.
Kilrush and Kilkee are two small towns on the west coast of Clare.
On the western shores of County Clare is the wonderfully varied Atlantic coastline with mighty cliffs, caverns and sandy bays. To the north the rugged coast rises 700 feet above the sea at the sheer Cliffs of Moher. Extending for over five miles these cliffs are home to puffins and guillemots, cormorants and rare fossils.
My favourite version of this ballad is by the Irish folk singer Christy Moore on his album "Prosperous" recorded in 1971.

It's a nice place to be on a fine summer's day
Watching all the wild flowers that ne'er do decay
Oh the hares and the pheasants are plain to be seen
Making homes for their young 'round the Cliffs of Doneen.

Take a view o'er the mountains, fine sights you'll see there
You'll see the high rocky mountains o'er the west coast of Clare
Oh the towns of Kilkee and Kilrush can be seen
From the high rocky slopes 'round the cliffs of Doneen.

Fare thee well to Doneen, fare thee well for a while
And to all the kind people I'm leaving behind
To the streams and the meadows where late I have been
And the high rocky slopes 'round the Cliffs of Doneen.

Fare thee well to Doneen, fare thee well for a while
And although we are parted by the raging sea wild
Once again I will walk with my Irish colleen
'Round the high rocky slopes of the Cliffs of Doneen.

The Meeting Of The Waters

This ballad was written by Thomas Moore (1779 – 1852), one of Ireland's greatest songwriters.

The air is an ancient Irish air "The Old Head of Denis" which is noted in George Petrie's "Ancient Music Of Ireland" (1855) in a slightly different version. Petrie says in the book that he collected this melody from the singing of Biddy Monaghan in Rathcarrick, County Sligo, in 1837.

Written in 1807 this ballad is about a village and vale in County Wicklow, south of Dublin on the easy coast, called Avoca, and the meeting of two rivers, the Avonmore and the Avonbeg. There are two meetings of these rivers in this vicinity – one at a place called Castle Howard and the other at Woodenbridge. Moore settled the question as to which of the scenes inspired his song in a letter to Lord John Russell in which he wrote "I believe the scene under Castle Howard was the one which suggested the song to me".

Below the Meeting Bridge is the stump of a tree known locally as 'Moore's tree' against which Moore is said to have often rested, contemplating the scene before him.

For further details about Thomas Moore and his songs see the Additional Notes at the front of this book.

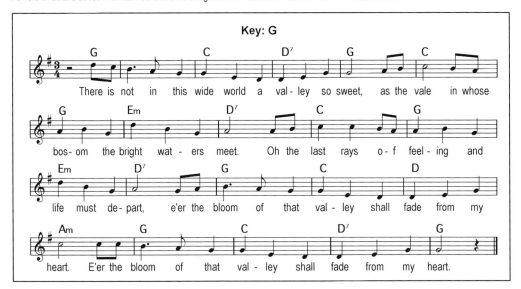

Yet it was not that Nature had shed o'er the scene
Her purest of crystal and brightest of green
'Twas not her soft magic of streamlet or hill
Oh no! It was something more exquisite still
Oh no! It was something more exquisite still.

'Twas that friends, the belov'd of my bosom were near
Who made every dear scene of enchantment more dear
And who felt how the best charms of Nature improve
When we see them reflected from looks that we love
When we see them reflected from looks that we love.

Sweet vale of Avoca how calm could I rest
In thy bosom of shade with the friends I love best
Where the storms that we feel in this cold world should cease
And our hearts like thy waters be mingled in peace
And our hearts like thy waters be mingled in peace.

The Jug Of Punch

This ballad was printed in "The Complete Collection Of Irish Music As Noted By George Petrie", published in 1903.
'Punch' is a mulled drink made up of a concoction of ingredients, but mainly alcohol. There can be several varieties of alcoholic drink mixed into the formula which can differ according to the tastes of its maker.
Naturally punch can be very potent! Because of its sweet taste and mulled properties there is a tendency to drink it quickly and in large amounts. Before you know where you are it can creep up on you and give you one hell of a wallop – hence the name! You've been warned - watch out!

What more diversion can a man desire than to sit him down by a snug coal fire
And upon his knee have a pretty wench and upon his table a jug of punch.
Chorus

If I was sickly and very bad and was not able for to go or stand
I would not think it at all amiss for to pledge my shoes for a jug of punch.
Chorus

The doctor fails with all his art to cure an impression on the heart
If life was gone but within an inch, what would bring it back but a jug of punch.
Chorus

But when I'm dead and within my grave no costly tombstone will I have
They'll dig a grave both wide and deep with a jug of punch at my head and feet.
Chorus

The Boys From The County Armagh

This is the County Anthem of all folk from County Armagh.
The County of Armagh is situated in the north east of Ireland. It is the smallest of the six counties of Northern Ireland.
The town of Armagh is the ecclesiastical capital of Ireland, the seat both of the Cardinal Archbishop and Catholic Primate of All Ireland, and the Protestant Archbishop. Hence the reference to "cathedral city".
The sacred Book of Armagh, one of Ireland's most precious heirlooms, can be seen in the Library of Trinity College Dublin. The book is a copy of the New Testament made for Abbot Torbach of Armagh in 807 by the master-scribe Ferdomnach. The book is of special interest to historians because it contains at the front a collection of 7th century texts about Saint Patrick and at the back a copy of the 4th century Life of Saint Martin of Tours.
Newtown, Forkhill, Crossmaglen and Blackwater are well known placenames and towns in County Armagh.

I've travelled that part of the county, through Newtown, Forkhill, Crossmaglen
Around by the gap of Mount Norris and home by Blackwater again
Where girls are so fair and so pretty; none better you'll find near or far
But where are the boys that can court them like the boys from the County Armagh! *Chorus*

I Once Loved A Lass

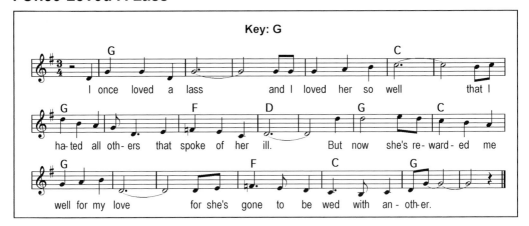

Key: G

I once loved a lass and I loved her so well that I
ha- ted all oth- ers that spoke of her ill. But now she's re- ward- ed me
well for my love for she's gone to be wed with an- oth- er.

When I saw my love walk through the church door
With groom and bride maidens they made a fine show
And I followed them in with my heart full of woe
For now she is wed to another.

When I saw my love sit down for to dine
I sat down beside her and poured out the wine
I drank to the lassie that should have been mine
But now she is wed to another.

The men in yon forest, they ask it of me
How many strawberries grow in the salt sea?
And I ask of them back with a tear in my eye
How many ships sail in the forest?

So dig me a grave and dig it so deep
And cover me over with flowers so sweet
And I will turn in for to take a long sleep
And maybe in time I'll forget her.

They dug him a grave and they dug it so deep
They covered him over with flowers so sweet
And he has turned in for to take a long sleep
And maybe by now he's forgotten.

The Raggle-Taggle Gypsy

This is an old ballad with many variation in Scotland, England and Ireland. Versions have been found back as far as 1720 under titles such as "Lady Cassillis Lilt", "Johnny Faa" and "The Gypsy Laddie". The earliest known printing of it was in "Tea Table Miscellany", a collection of English and Scottish ballads in three volumes edited by the Scottish poet Allan Ramsay (1686 – 1758).
In the late 18th century this ballad was associated with John, the sixth Earl of Cassilis and his first wife Lady Jean Hamilton. Before her marriage to the Earl in the early 1600's, Jean Hamilton was in love with a gypsy, Johnny Faa of Dunbar. In later years when the Earl and Lady Jean had settled into normal domestic life, Johnny Faa returned and persuaded her to elope. Johnny Faa was hanged for this indiscretion in 1624 and Lady Jean was banished for life to a tower constructed specifically for her imprisonment. You didn't mess around in those days!

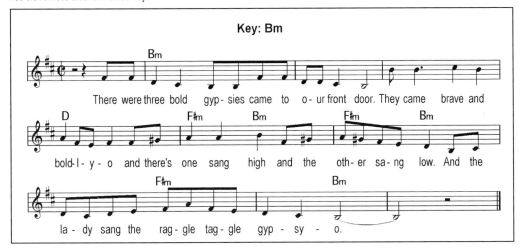

They sang sweet and they sang low and fast her tears began to flow
She laid down her silken gown her golden rings and all her show.

It was upstairs and downstairs the lady went; put on her suit of leather-o
And it was the cry all around the door "She's away with the raggle-taggle gypsy-o".

It was late that night when the lord came home enquiring for his lady-o
The servant's voice rang around the house; "She is gone with the raggle-taggle gypsy-o".

"Oh then saddle for me, my milk white steed; the black horse is not speedy-o
And I will ride and I'll seek me bride whose away with the raggle-taggle gypsy-o".

Oh then he rode high and he rode low; he rode north and south also
But when he came to a wide open field it is there that he spotted his lady-o.

"Oh then why did you leave your house and your land; why did you leave your money-o
And why did you leave your newly wedded lord to be off with the raggle-taggle gypsy-o".

"Yerra what do I care for me house and me land and what do I care for money-o
And what do I care for my newly-wedded lord; I'm away with the raggle-taggle gypsy-o".

"And what do I care for my goose-feathered bed with blankets drawn so comely-o
Tonight I'll sleep in the wide open field all along with the raggle-taggle gypsy-o".

"Oh for you rode east when I rode west; you rode high and I rode low
I'd rather have a kiss from the yellow gypsy's lips than all your land and money-o".

The Jolly Beggarman

The air of this old ballad is thought to have originated in Scotland, the 'Jolly Beggarman' being King James V of Scotland. James V (1513 – 1545) had a reputation for wandering around in the disguise of a vagrant and chasing innocent unsuspecting maidens. The lyrics first appeared in print in the 1730's in England.

He would not lie within the barn nor yet within the byre
But he would in the corner lie down by the kitchen fire
And then the beggar's bed was made of good clean sheets and hay
And down beside the kitchen fire the jolly beggar lay. ***Chorus***

The farmer's daughter she got up to bolt the kitchen door
And there she saw the beggar standing naked on the floor
He took the daughter in his arms and to the bed he ran
"Kind sir", she said "Be easy now, you'll waken our good man". ***Chorus***

"O no, you are no beggar man, you are some gentleman
For you have stole my maidenhead and I am quite undone"
"I am no lord, I am no squire, of beggars I be one
And beggars they be robbers all and you are quite undone". ***Chorus***

The farmer's wife came down the stairs, awakened from her sleep
She saw the beggar and the girl and she began to weep
She took the bed in both her hands and threw it at the wall
Saying "Go you with the beggar man, your maidenhead and all!". ***Chorus***

108

Weile Walia

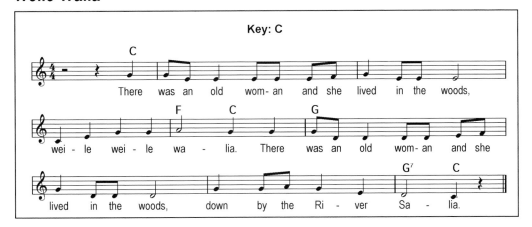

She had a baby three months old, weile, weile, walia
She had a baby three months old, down by the River Salia.

She had a pen-knife long and sharp, weile, weile, walia
She had a pen-knife long and sharp, down by the River Salia.

She stuck the pen-knife in the baby's heart, weile, weile, walia
She stuck the pen-knife in the baby's heart, down by the River Salia.

Three loud knocks came a-knocking on the door, weile, weile, walia
Three loud knocks came a-knocking on the door, down by the River Salia.

Two policemen and a man, weile, weile, walia
Two policemen and a man, down by the River Salia.

"Are you the woman that killed the child", weile, weile, walia
"Are you the woman that killed the child", down by the River Salia.

They tied her hands behind her back, weile, weile, walia
They tied her hands behind her back, down by the River Salia.

The rope was pulled and she got hung, weile, weile walia
The rope was pulled and she got hung, down by the River Salia.

And that was the end of the woman in the woods, weile, weile, walia
And that was the end of the baby too, down by the River Salia.

The Rose Of Allendale

This is also known as "The Rose Of Allandale" and was written by Sidney Nelson and Charles Jefferys.
I can't find Allendale (or Allandale) anywhere in Ireland.

Where e'er I wandered, east or west; though fate began to lour
A solace still she was to me in sorrow's lonely hour
When tempests lashed our lonesome barque and tore her shiv'ring sail
One maiden form withstood the storm; 'twas the Rose of Allendale.
Chorus

And when my fevered lips were parched on Africa's hot sands
She whispered hopes of happiness and tales of distant lands
My life has been a wilderness, unblessed by fortune's gale
Had fate not linked my lot to hers, the Rose of Allendale.
Chorus

Danny Boy

This ballad has often been referred to as "The Derry Air" or, more geographically correct, "The Londonderry Air".
Undoubtedly one of the most popular ballads to be heard in the kitchens and pubs of Ireland!
It is also one of the most consistently murdered ballads I know, because amateur balladeers usually start singing it in too high a pitch for their voice realising (when it is too late!) that they can't reach the high E note in the chorus. Keep that in mind – don't get caught out!
The air of this ballad is called "The Londonderry Air" (or more simply, "The Derry Air"). However, as there are over 100 songs composed to that air it is more correct to call it "Danny Boy". (Thomas Moore composed a song to this air, called "My Gentle Harp".) The air first appeared in print in "Ancient Music of Ireland" (1855) by the collector George Petrie in which he gratefully thanks a Miss J. Ross of Newtown-Limavady in County Derry (Northern Ireland) for bringing the song to his attention. He also states that "the name of the tune unfortunately was not ascertained by Miss Ross, who sent it to me with the simple remark that it was 'very old', in the correctness of which statement I have no hesitation in expressing my perfect concurrence". Thus it was baptised "The Derry Air".
However as no additional versions of the melody were ever reported by any of the other folk collectors there is speculation that Miss Ross may have composed the air herself but for some reason didn't wish to claim credit for it. The speculation still continues.
The lyrics of Danny Boy were written by an English lawyer, Frederic Edward Weatherly (1848 – 1929). In 1910 he wrote the lyrics and music for an unsuccessful song he called 'Danny Boy'. However in 1912 his sister-in-law sent him the score of 'The Derry Air' from America and he immediately noticed that his Danny Boy lyrics perfectly fitted the melody.
In 1913 he published the song in its new form.

And when ye come and all the flowers are dying; and if I'm dead, as dead I well may be
You'll come and find the place where I am lying; and kneel and say an 'Avé' there for me. *Chorus*

And I shall hear, though soft you tread above me; and all my grave will warmer, sweeter be
If you will bend and tell me that you love me; then I shall sleep in peace till you're with me. *Chorus*

Come To The Bower

This is a patriotic ballad, made famous by recordings by The Clancy Brothers and also The Dubliners.

It is a call to all Irishmen abroad to return to Ireland and take Ireland back from the English occupiers. Consequently there are many references in this ballad to great and heroic deeds of Irishmen in the past, designed to stir up the blood of all Irish people abroad.

"O'Neill" refers to Hugh O'Neill (1550 – 1616), Earl of Tyrone. "O'Donnell" refers to 'Red Hugh' O'Donnell (1572 – 1602) Lord of Tirconnell (see page 32). "Lord Lucan" refers to the patriot leader Patrick Sarsfield, Earl of Lucan (1655 – 1693). "O'Connell" refers to Daniel O'Connell (1775 – 1847) who secured Catholic emancipation from the Penal Laws and is know as 'The Liberator'. "Brian drove the Danes" refers to Brian Boru, High King of Ireland, whose army defeated the Danes at the Battle of Clontarf in 1014. "Benburb" refers to the Battle of Benburb which took place near the town of Benburb in County Tyrone in 1646, a battle between the Irish under Owen Roe O'Neill and the Scottish under General Munroe. 3000 Scottish troops were slain and the Irish losses amounted to only 40. It was an overwhelming victory for the Irish.

"Blackwater" refers to Blackwatertown in County Armagh, whose English garrison was successfully blockaded by Hugh O'Neill in 1598. "Dungannon" refers to the town of Dungannon, County Tyrone, site of the ancient fortress of the O'Neill clan.

New Ross, Wexford and Gorey are towns in County Wexford which saw scenes of fierce fighting and bloodshed during the 1798 Rebellion. (For further information about the 1798 Rebellion see the Additional Notes at the front of this book.)

A 'bower' is a shady and hidden enclosure or recess in a garden, indicating that the singer of this ballad wants all Irishmen to meet with him in a secret location to plan the overthrow of the English forces in Ireland.

Will you come to the land of O'Neill and O'Donnell
Of Lord Lucan of old and immortal O'Connell
Where Brian drove the Danes and St. Patrick the vermin
And whose valleys remain still most beautiful and charming. *Chorus*

You can visit Benburb and the storied Blackwater
Where Owen Roe met Munroe and his chieftains did slaughter
You may ride on the tide o'er the broad majestic Shannon
You may sail 'round Lough Neagh and see storied Dungannon. *Chorus*

You can visit New Ross, gallant Wexford and Gorey
Where the green was last seen by proud Saxon and Tory
Where the soil is sanctified by the blood of each true man
Where they died, satisfied, their enemies they would not run from. *Chorus*

Will you come and awake our lost land from its slumbers
And her fetters we will break; links that long are encumbered
And the air will resound with 'Hosannas' to greet you
On the shore will be found gallant Irishmen to meet you. *Chorus*

~~~~~~~~~~~~~~

The Gypsy

You met me at the marketplace when your ma was not with you
You liked my long brown ringlets and my handkerchief of blue
Although I'm very fond of you and you asked me home to tea
I am a gypsy rover and you can't come with me.
Chorus

Your brother is a peeler and he would put me in jail
If he knew I was a poacher and I hunt your lord's best game
Your daddy is a gentleman, your mammy's just as grand
But I'm a gypsy rover; I'll not be your husband.
Chorus

The hour is drawing on my love and your ma's expecting thee
Don't you say you met me here for I'm just a gypsy
Please let go my jacket now; your love will have to wait
For I am twenty-two years old and you are only eight.
Chorus

As I Roved Out

This old ballad has a question-and-answer pattern which is often found with older types of Anglo-Scots 'riddling' ballads. There is an old Scots ballad entitled 'The Trooper And The Maid' with a very similar theme and lyrics.

My two favourite versions of this ballad are by the traditional group Planxty on their CD "Planxty" and also by The Woods Band on their album "The Woods Band" (1971).

"And will you come to my mother's house when the moon is shining clearly (repeat)
I'll open the door and I'll let you in and divil the one will hear us". *Chorus*

So I went to her house in the middle of the night when the moon was shining clearly (repeat)
And she opened the door and she let me in and divil the one did hear us. *Chorus*

She took my horse by the bridle and the bit and she led him to the stable (repeat)
Saying "There's plenty of oats for a soldier's horse to eat them if he's able". *Chorus*

Then she took me by the lily-white hand and she led me to the table (repeat)
Saying "There's plenty of wine for the soldier boy to drink it if your able". *Chorus*

I got up and I made me bed and I made it nice and easy (repeat)
Then I took her up and I laid her down saying "Lassie are you able?" *Chorus*

And there we lay till the breaking of the day and divil the one did hear us (repeat)
Then I arose and put on my clothes, saying "Lassie, I must leave you". *Chorus*

"And when will you return again and when will we be married?" (repeat)
"When broken shells make Christmas bells, then will we be married". *Chorus*

Henry My Son

The earliest printed version of this ballad is in 1787 in "The Scots Musical Museum" published by the collector James Johnson. It was printed under the title "Lord Ronald, My Son".
This ballad is found throughout Ireland, Britain and North America and is also known as "Lord Randall", "Jimmy Randal" and "Jimmy Randolph".
It has been suggested that this ballad is associated with the death of Thomas Randolph (Randal) Earl of Moray who died in 1332. Speculation has it that he may have been poisoned by his wife.
There is a German version called "Grossmutter-Schlangenkoechin" where the boy dies following a bite from a poisonous snake.
The air has also been found in many countries on the European mainland.

And what did you have to eat, Henry my son
What did you have to eat, my beloved one
Poisoned beads, poisoned beads.
Chorus

What colour were those beads, Henry my son
What colour were those beads, my beloved one
Green and yellow, green and yellow.
Chorus

What will you leave your mother, Henry my son
What will you leave your mother, my beloved one
A woollen blanket, a woollen blanket.
Chorus

What will you leave your children, Henry my son
What will you leave your children, my beloved one
The keys of heaven, the keys of heaven.
Chorus

And what will you leave your sweetheart, Henry my son
What will you leave your sweetheart, my beloved one
A rope to hang her, a rope to hang her.
Chorus

The Bard Of Armagh

This ballad is also known as "Brady's Lament".
The County of Armagh is situated in the north-east of Ireland. It is the smallest of the six counties of Northern Ireland.
County Wexford is situated in the south-east of Ireland. I can't find any "Durrish" in Ireland but there is a small village in County Cork called Durrus so this may be the place referred to by Bold Phelim Brady.
The air of this ballad was also used in the popular American country song "The Streets of Laredo".
There is another ballad in this book with connections to Armagh. See "The Boys from the County Armagh" - page 105.

When I was a young lad King Jamie did flourish
And I followed the wars with my brogues bound with straw
And all the fair colleens from Wexford to Durrish
Called me Bold Phelim Brady, the Bard of Armagh.

How I love for to muse on the days of my boyhood
Though four score and three years have flitted since then
Still it gives sweet reflections as every young joy should
For light-hearted boys make the best of old men.

At pattern or fair I could twist my shillelagh
Or trip through a jig with me brogues bound with straw
Whilst all the pretty maidens around me assembled
For Bold Phelim Brady, the Bard of Armagh.

Although I have travelled this wide world all over
But Erin's my home and a parent to me
Then oh, let the ground that my old bones will cover
Be cut from the soil that is trod by the free.

And when Sergeant Death in his arms shall embrace me
Oh lull me to sleep with sweet 'Erin go Brath'*
By the side of my young wife, dear Kathleen, oh place me
Then forget Phelim Brady, the Bard of Armagh.

*Pronounced "Erin go bra" (Ireland forever!)

The Glendalough Saint

(Verses and chorus have the same melody)

Glendalough is perhaps one of the most picturesque of the glens in County Wicklow, about 35 miles from Dublin city. It derives its name from the Irish 'Gleann Da Loch' meaning 'the valley of the two lakes'.
Early in the 6th century Saint Kevin came to this quiet place to live the life of a hermit, firstly on the shores of the north side of the Upper Lake and later in a narrow cave on the south side accessible only by boat. Numbers of followers were attracted by his saintly reputation. To meet the spiritual needs of these followers he built a church on the south side of the Upper Lake. However the number of followers increased to such an extent that he moved to the lower part of the glen and founded a monastery there which flourished for six centuries. Much of the ruins of this monastery are still preserved to this day, and Glendalough is a favourite destination for foreign visitors and Irish people alike, not only for the beauty of the place but also for its serenity.
So how this story of the saint and a woman called Kathleen ever came about is anyone's guess!
This ballad was made famous by a recording of it by the Irish folk group, The Dubliners.

Fol-ol di lol-lol di lol-lay; fol-ol di lol-lol di lol-laddy
Fol-ol di lol-lol di lol-lay; fol-ol di lol-lol di lol-laddy

He was fond of reading a book when he could get one to his wishes
He was fond of casting his hook down among the young fishes.
Chorus

One day he caught him a fish; he caught himself a fine trout, sir
When Kathleen from over the lake came to see what the monk was about, sir.
Chorus

"Get out of me way" said the saint for I am a man of great piety
And me good manners I wouldn't taint to be mixing with female society.
Chorus

Oh but Kathleen she wouldn't give in and when he went home to his rockery
He found she was seated therein a-polishing up his old crockery.
Chorus

Well he gave the poor creature a shake and I wish that the peelers had caught him
For he flung her right into the lake and begorra she sank to the bottom!
Chorus

Banna Strand

Banna Strand is on the shores of County Kerry in the south-east of Ireland.

This song relates to a famous and fateful incident which took place during the lead-up to the Easter Rising of 1916 and involved the Irish patriot, Sir Roger Casement (1864 – 1916).

Born in Sandycove, County Dublin into an Ulster Protestant family, Casement joined the British Colonial Service in 1892. He won international acclaim for his courageous reports on the exploitation of native workers by the rubber planters in the Belgian Congo and the Putamayo area of Peru. He received a knighthood for his achievements in 1911 and retired from the Colonial Services in 1913.

Casement was an Irish Nationalist at heart and was involved in the foundation of the Irish Volunteers. He firmly believed that an uprising against Britain could not be successful without German assistance.

In 1914 he travelled to Berlin to seek aid from the Germans for an uprising in Ireland against Britain. The German authorities agreed to send a shipload of arms and ammunition to Ireland and Casement set sail aboard the 'Aud', bound for Ireland, on April 9th, 1916.

When she arrived off the coast of Kerry the 'Aud' was to receive a signal from land and thus would commence the unloading of the valuable cargo. But no signal came. The arrangement was that two green fishing lamps would give the signal from land.

These lamps had been collected in Dublin three weeks earlier and were hanging in the Volunteer's drill-hall in Tralee.

The local Volunteer leaders had been told by Dublin that the 'Aud' would not arrive before the evening of Easter Sunday, April 23rd.

However the 'Aud' arrived on Holy Thursday and waited anxiously and in vain for a signal from shore. As the Irish coastline was being extensively patrolled by the British Navy it was only a matter of time before she would raise suspicions.

After a few close encounters during which the captain of the 'Aud', Lieutenant Karl Spindler, successfully bluffed his adversaries, the captain of a British Navy sloop, 'Bluebell', became suspicious of this strange vessel lurking about in Tralee Bay and ordered the 'Aud' to accompany her to Cobh to be searched. Knowing he could not out-run 'Bluebell' Spindler scuttled his ship outside Cobh Harbour. The 20,000 rifles, 1 million rounds of ammunition and 10 machine guns (part of the spoils of Hindenburg's victory over the Russians at Tannenberg) sank with her to the bottom of the sea.

The real blame for this calamity must be directed at the leaders of the Rising and the German Admiralty. Originally the leaders requested that the arms be delivered sometime between Holy Thursday and Easter Monday and the Germans agreed to this. However in early April the leaders became concerned that, if the arms were to arrive on Holy Thursday, the British authorities would probably know all about the operation well before the start of the Rising and the vital element of surprise would be lost. They decided to change the plans and requested that the arms should not arrive until sometime after Easter Sunday.

As the First World War was still raging at the time direct communications between the United Kingdom (which included Ireland) and Germany was impossible, so the message to alter the landing arrangements was carried by a nationalist sympathiser to John Devoy, head of Clan na Gael in New York. He would then relay it to Germany.

In the meantime, satisfied that the change of plans would be successfully relayed to the Germans, the leaders of the Rising informed the Tralee Volunteers that the arms would not arrive until sometime after Easter Sunday.

However, the emissary did not arrive in New York until April 14th, and the 'Aud' had departed for Ireland five days earlier. When Devoy contacted the German Admiralty with the altered plans he was informed that there was no radio on board the 'Aud' and therefore they couldn't change the landing arrangements. Although Devoy vehemently insisted that he sent an urgent message back to Dublin to this effect, there is no record of any such message and the leaders of the Rising continued to plan as if the arms landing schedule had been altered.

And the Tralee Volunteers still continued to make their own plans under the erroneous assumption that the arms would not arrive until after Easter Sunday.

While the 'Aud' was anxiously waiting for a signal from the shore Casement had landed at Banna Strand in a small boat from the accompanying German submarine 'U.19'. On Good Friday he was arrested by two suspicious Royal Irish Constabulary officers at a prehistoric site known locally as McKenna's Fort.

The failure to land the ammunition and the subsequent arrest of Casement inspired Eoin McNeill, the Commander-in-Chief of the Irish Volunteers, to immediately cancel the plans for the 1916 Rising. He was considerably successful in his endeavours as only a handful of Volunteers turned out for 'manoeuvres' on Easter Monday.

Roger Casement was convicted of treason and hanged in Pentonville Prison, London, in August 1916. His trial for treason attracted world-wide attention.

Following on extensive negotiations between the Irish and British Governments Casement's remains were returned to Ireland in 1965 where he was honoured with a State Funeral.

For further information about the Easter Rising see the Additional Notes at the front of this book.

Key: D

'Twas on Good Fri - day mo - rn - ing all in the month of May. A Ger - man ship was sig - nal-ing be- yond out in the bay. With twen - ty thous- and ri - fl - es all rea - dy for to land. But no ans - wering sig - nal did come from the lone - ly Ban - na Strand

"No signal answers from the shore" Sir Roger sadly said
"No comrades here to meet me; alas they must be dead
But I must do my duty and today I mean to land"
So in a small boat rowed ashore on the lonely Banna Strand.

The R.I.C*. were hunting for Sir Roger high and low
They found him in McKenna's Fort; said they "You are our foe"
Said he "I'm Roger Casement, I come to my native land
And I mean to free my countrymen on the lonely Banna Strand"

They took Sir Roger prisoner and sailed to London Town
And in the Tower they locked him up; a traitor to the Crown
Said he "I am no traitor" but on trial he had to stand
For bringing German rifles to the lonely Banna Strand.

'Twas in an English prison that they led him to his death
"I'm dying for my country" he said with his last breath
They buried him in British soil far from his native land
And the wild waves sang his requiem on the lonely Banna Strand.

*Royal Irish Constabulary

The Shores Of Americay

This is a ballad about emigration.

Most Irishmen and women emigrated because of necessity. See "Skibbereen" – page 56. However the writer of this ballad is not leaving because of economic necessity, but rather to carve out a new life for his beloved and himself in America.

The sentiments in this ballad are not unlike those expressed in "Muirsheen Durkin" (page 94).

It is estimated that at least 8 million Irish men and women emigrated from Ireland between 1801 and 1921 and many more left during the depression years of the 20th century. The statement, therefore, by President Mary Robinson in December 1990, that there are at least 70 million people throughout the world who claim to be of Irish descent, is not an exaggeration.

The most common destination for Irish emigrants prior to the 1860's was Canada; between then and the First World War it was the U.S.A., and from then on it was Great Britain.

And it's not for the want of employment I go, and it's not for the love of fame
Or that fortune so bright may shine over me and give me a glorious name
No it's not for the want of employment I go o'er the stormy and perilous sea
But to seek a new home for my own true love on the shores of Americay.

And when I am bidding my final farewell the teardrops like rain will blind
To think of my friends in my own native land and the home that I'm leaving behind
And If I'm to die in a foreign land and be buried so distant away
No fond mother's tears will be shed o'er my grave on the shores of Americay.

The Nightingale

(Verses and chorus have the same melody)

This ballad is probably of English origin and is also known as "The Bold Grenadier". The words and sentiments are also very similar to several verses of a ballad which was printed in 1675 by W. Olney of London entitled "The Nightingale's Song: Or The Soldier's Rare Musick, And The Maid's Recreation" to be found in the Bodleian Library in Oxford University. The broadside says that it is to be sung to the melody of "No, No, Not I".
There is also another very popular and quite different English ballad called "The Nightingale" which begins with the line 'My love he was a rich farmer's son'.
The romantic nightingale is a long distance migrant cousin of the familiar garden Robin. It is only active on these islands for a few weeks in late Spring. The most unique feature of this bird is, of course, that it sings at night-time and has therefore gained a reputation as a bird of romance. Its chirp or voice is very varied and noted for its contralto qualities with whistles and haunting repeated phrases.
We Irish would have quite an affiliation to the nightingale. You mightn't see us very much during the day but at night-time we can be heard singing over long distances! There is one subtle difference between ourselves and these beautiful birds, however – we tend to consume lots of beer in the course of our singing (indeed very often that is the principal reason for our singing in the first place). I don't think that the nightingale partakes in that activity!

And they kissed so sweet and comforting as they clung to each other
They went arm-in-arm along the road like sister and brother
They went arm-in-arm along the road till they came to a stream
And they both sat down together for to hear the nightingale sing.

From out of his knapsack he took a fine fiddle
And he played her such a merry tune with a hi-diddle-diddle
And he played her such a merry tune that the trees they did ring
And they both sat down together for to hear the nightingale sing. *Chorus*

Oh soldier, handsome soldier will you marry me
Oh no said the soldier that never can be
For I have a wife at home in my own country
And she is the sweetest little flower that you ever did see. *Chorus*

Now I am off to India for seven long years
Drinking wine and strong whiskey instead of cold beers
And if ever I return again it will be in the spring
And we'll both sit down together for to hear the nightingale sing. *Chorus*

Sam Hall

This old ballad also goes under the title of "Jack Hall" and probably relates to a chimney sweep named Jack Hall who was a well-known burglar. He was hanged for his crimes in 1701.
In the 1850's a music hall entertainer, C.W. Ross, gained quite a reputation for singing a bawdy version of this ballad.
There is another English ballad with the same rhythm and word pattern called "Captain Kidd" who ironically was hanged for piracy in London in the same year as Jack Hall.

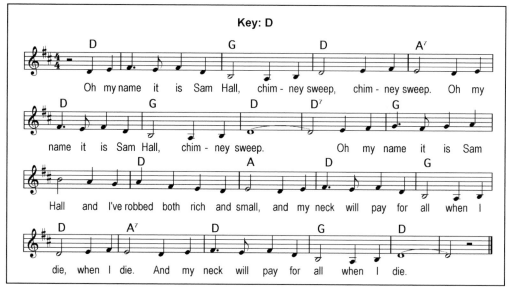

Oh they took me to Coote Hill in a cart, in a cart
Oh they took me to Coote Hill in a cart
Oh they took me to Coote Hill and 'twas there I made my will
For the best of friends must part; so must I, so must I
For the best of friends must part; so must I.

Now the preacher he did come, he did come, he did come
Of the preacher he did come, he did come
Oh the preacher he did come and he looked so doggone glum
And he talked of Kingdom Come with a tear, with a tear
And he talked of Kingdom Come with a tear.

Up the ladder I did grope; that's no joke, that's no joke
Up the ladder I did grope; that's no joke
Up the ladder I did grope and the hangman pulled the rope
And ne'er a word I spoke; tumbling down, tumbling down
And ne'er a word I spoke; tumbling down.

(Repeat first verse)

Old Woman From Wexford

I've come across this ballad in various different forms both in Ireland and England. The oldest printed version is called "Old Woman From Blighter Town" but there are also versions in England where the old woman is from Yorkshire or Dover.
There is a version entitled "Tipping It Up To Nancy" (page 125) recorded by the Irish folk singer Christy Moore on his first album "Paddy on the Road" in 1969.
I've never tried eating 'eggs and marrowbones' so I couldn't tell you whether or not the potion works!
County Wexford is in the south-eastern corner of Ireland with a long coastline on both the Irish Sea and the Celtic Sea. On the north it is bounded by the hill of County Wicklow and on the west by the River Barrow and the Blackstairs Mountains.
Wexford played host to King Henry II in 1172 when he came over from England to Selskar Abbey to do penance for the murder of Thomas á Becket. It is also well-known as the birthplace of the family of the former American President, John F. Kennedy.

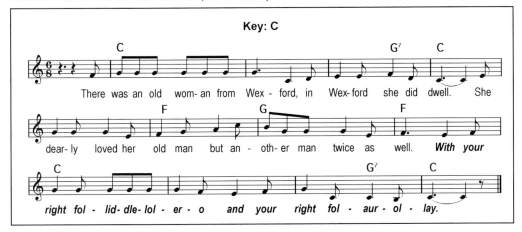

One day she went to the doctor for some medicine for to find
Says she "Will ye give me something for to make me old man blind". *Chorus*

"Feed him eggs and marrowbones and make him suck them all
And it won't be very long before he won't see you at all". *Chorus*

The doctor wrote a letter and he signed it with his hand
And he sent it to the old man so that he would understand. *Chorus*

She fed him eggs and marrowbones and made him suck them all
And it wasn't very long before he couldn't see the wall. *Chorus*

Said he "I'd like to drown myself but that would be a sin"
Said she "I'll come along with you and help to push you in". *Chorus*

The woman she stepped back a bit to rush and push him in
But the old man quickly stepped aside and she went tumbling in. *Chorus*

How loudly she did holler oh how loudly she did call
"Yerra hold your whist old woman sure I can't see you at all". *Chorus*

Now eggs and eggs and marrowbones may make your old man blind
But if you want to drown him you must creep up from behind. *Chorus*

All For Me Grog

(Verses and chorus have the same melody)

This very popular ballad was recorded some years ago by the Irish folk group, The Dubliners.
In the song the singer is lamenting the fact that he has spent all of his money on the three pastimes much favoured by many's an Irishman – Wine, Women and Song (or, as some cruder folk would have it – 'Booze, Birds and Ballads').
There are other versions of this ballad – "My Jolly Jolly Tar" (1904) and "The Nobby Hat" (1906). The ballad is also know as "Here's To The Grog".
'Grog' was a mixture of rum and water but the name gradually became a term for alcohol in general.
Grog was served as a ration in the United States Navy until 1862, and in the British Navy until 1970.

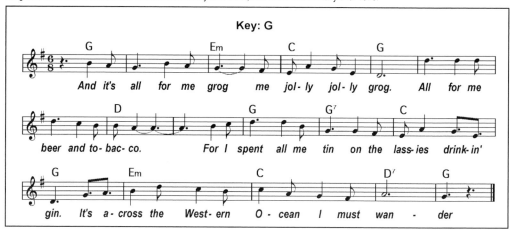

Where are me boots, me noggin' noggin' boots
They're all gone for beer and tobacco
For the heels are worn out and the toes are kicked about
And the soles are lookin' out for better weather.
Chorus

Where is me shirt, me noggin' noggin' shirt
It's all gone for beer and tobacco
For the collar is all worn and the sleeves they are all torn
And the tail is lookin' out for better weather.
Chorus

I'm sick in the head and I haven't been to bed
Since I first came ashore from me slumber
For I spent all me dough on the lassies, don't you know
Far across the Western Ocean I must wander.
Chorus

Tipping It Up To Nancy

See "The Old Woman From Wexford" - page 123 for another completely different version of this song.

She went down to the chemist shop some remedies for to find
"Have you anything in your chemist shop to make me old man blind?"
Chorus

"Give him eggs and marrowbones and make him suck them all
And before he has the last one sucked he won't see you at all".
Chorus

She gave him eggs and marrowbones and made him suck them all
Before he had the last one sucked he couldn't see the wall.
Chorus

"If in this world I cannot see, then here I cannot stay
"I'd rather go and drown meself"; says she "I'll show the way".
Chorus

She led him to the river and she led him to the brim
But sly enough of the old lad it was him that shoved her in.
Chorus

"Oh husband dear I'm going to drown don't leave me here behind!"
"Yerra shut your mouth" the old lad said, "sure don't ye know I'm blind".
Chorus

Boulavogue

This fine ballad was written by Patrick Joseph McCall (1861 – 1919).

P.J. McCall was born in Dublin in 1861. His works, "Fenian Nights Entertainments", told the stories of the Irish heroes and carried on the work of "The Nation" (see page 98) in educating the Irish people about their history and heritage. He died in Dublin in 1919.

This emotive ballad and another called "Kelly from Killane" (also written by McCall - page 96) were both written in 1898 to mark the centenary of the 1798 rebellion.

"Boulavogue" is regarded by many (including myself) as the anthem of the 1798 Rebellion in Wexford. It sets out a brief history of the rebellion which took place in the Wexford area using the exploits of Father John Murphy (c. 1753 – 1798) of Boulavogue, County Wexford as its main theme.

Father Murphy was curate of Boulavogue and was one of the leaders of the 1798 rebellion in the south-east, although he was not a member of the United Irishmen. The proper Ordnance Survey spelling of the village is 'Boleyvogue' and it is situated about eight miles north-east of Enniscorthy.

Father Murphy was born near Ferns in County Wexford. Originally he was against the idea of a rebellion encouraged his parishioners to surrender any weapons in their possession. However, when his church was burned by the North Cork militia on May 26th, along with about twenty cottages belonging to local farming families, he rapidly altered his opinion.

Motivated by the reports of atrocities committed by Government forces and loyalists at Dunlavin and Carnew, Father Murphy agreed to lead the local insurgents into revolt.

On the evening of May 26th a patrol of yeomen from the nearby town of Camolin was sent to a farmhouse near the village of Harrow to search for arms. They were under the command of a local gentleman loyal to the Crown by the name of Lieutenant Bookey. This patrol found their way blocked outside Harrow by Father Murphy's men. In the ensuing skirmish Bookey and his assistant were killed and the remaining yeomen fled. Father Murphy then sent a party of his men to raid the house of Lord Mountnorris at Camolin where there was a large stockpile of arms. Mountnorris was not in residence at the time and the insurgents plundered the house without interruption.

As local Government forces quickly closed in on his men Father Murphy decided to make a stand on Oulart Hill. Although ill-armed against the North Cork militia under the command of Colonel Foote the insurgents achieved a decisive victory at Oulart Hill on May 27th. They then marched on and captured the undefended town of Ferns and on May 28th captured Enniscorthy. However their luck changed on June 9th when Father Murphy's forces suffered a serious defeat at the Battle of Arklow with the loss of about three hundred men.

The Crown forces gradually regained control and following the defeat of the insurgents on June 21st 1798 at the Battle of Vinegar Hill, near Enniscorthy town, Father Murphy was captured at Tullow, Co. Carlow and hanged.

A "yeoman" was a member of a part-time local force established in 1796. It was composed of men loyal to the English crown and comprised mainly Protestant landowners and merchants. The force gained a reputation for indiscriminate and undisciplined sectarian violence.

"Tubberneering" and "Ballyellis" are places in Wexford where battles occurred during the Rising. "Enniscorthy", traversed by the River Slaney, is a large town in Wexford which was taken by the insurgents in May 1798 but was recaptured by the English forces at the decisive Battle of Vinegar Hill.

For further information on the 1798 rebellion see the Additional Notes at the front of this book.

He led us on 'gainst the coming soldiers and the cowardly yeomen we put to flight
'Twas at the Harrow the boys of Wexford showed Bookey's regiment how men could fight
Look out for hirelings King George of England; search every kingdom where breathes a slave
For Father Murphy of County Wexford sweeps o'er the land like a mighty wave.

We took Camolin and Enniscorthy and Wexford, storming, drove out our foes
'Twas at Slieve Coilte our pikes were reeking with crimson blood of the beaten Yoes
At Tubberneering and Ballyellis full many a Hessian lay in his gore
Ah, Father Murphy, had aid come over, the Green Flag floated from shore to shore

At Vinegar Hill o'er the pleasant Slaney our heroes vainly stood back to back
And the Yeos of Tullow took Father Murphy and burned his body upon the rack
God grant you glory brave Father Murphy and open heaven to all your men
The cause that called you may call tomorrow in another fight for the Green again

The Lark In The Morning

The lark (or to use its official name 'Skylark', or *alauda arvensis*) is a very common bird in Ireland. It is estimated that over one million skylarks breed in Ireland each year. Their favourite habitats are the open country and coastal dunes. They make their nests on the ground, usually under clumps of tall grass. They often perch and sing on fence posts.

One of the great characteristics of skylarks is their practice of flying at high altitude especially over stubble fields where they find most of their food – cereal grain and insects.

The lark is one of the first birds to be heard in the morning in open countryside – hence they have become symbolic of the morning and the dawn of a new day. Its continuous song consists of a constant jumble of twittering, chirping and warbling sounds, often including the imitation of other song birds. It sings as it ascends into the heavens and hovers on fluttering wings, sometimes until it is almost out of sight.

There is another song in this book relating to the skylark. See "My Singing Bird" - page 23.

Oh Roger the ploughboy he is a dashing blade
He goes whistling and singing in yonder leafy shade
He met with dark-eyed Susan; she's handsome I declare
And she is far more enticing than the birds all in the air.

As they were coming home from the rakes of the town
The meadow being all mown and the grass had been cut down
And as they should chance to tumble all in the new-mown hay
"Oh, it's kiss me now or never" this bonnie lass would say

When twenty long weeks were over and had passed
Her mammy asked the reason why she thickened 'round the waist
"It was the pretty ploughboy" this lassie then did say
"For he asked me for to tumble all in the new-mown hay"

Here's a health to you ploughboys wherever you may be
That like to have a bonnie lass a-sitting on each knee
With a pint of good strong porter he'll whistle and he'll sing
And the ploughboy is as happy as a prince or as a king

The Rocks Of Bawn

In this ballad the singer tells of the wretched plight of the farm labourer, and he wishes that the Recruiting Sergeant would recruit him into the army so that he would escape the misery of working for a miserly farmer. In the first verse he warns all potential labourers to be very careful when they are making their bargains at the hiring fair.

The hiring of farm labour through the hiring fairs was very common during the late 19th century. At these fairs farmers and those seeking work would negotiate wages and conditions of work. They were most popular in Ulster (Northern Ireland) and were usually held twice a year – in May and November. Working contracts were for a six month period.

The largest fairs were held in the Ulster towns of Derry, Strabane, Letterkenny and Omagh.

The hiring fairs began to disappear at the beginning of the 20th century and for a while many of them evolved into social occasions and local festivals.

My shoes they are all worn and my stockings they are thin
My heart is always trembling now for fear they might give in
My heart is always trembling now from the clear daylight till the dawn
And I never will be able to plough the Rocks of Bawn.

My curse upon you Sweeney boy, you have me nearly robbed
You're sitting by the fireside now, your feet upon the hob
You're sitting by the fireside now from the clear daylight till the dawn
And you never will be able to plough the Rocks of Bawn

Rise up gallant Sweeney, and get your horses hay
And give them a good feed of oats before they start away
Don't feed them on soft turnip sprigs that grow on yon green lawn
Or they never will be able to plough the Rocks of Bawn.

I wish the Sergeant-Major would send for me in time
And place me in some regiment while in my youth and prime
I'd fight for Ireland's glory now from the clear daylight till the dawn
Before I would return again to plough the Rocks of Bawn.

The Rose Of Mooncoin

(Verses and chorus have the same melody)

This is the County Anthem of all the Kilkenny people around the world and was written by Seamus Kavanagh who has written other Irish ballads such as "Moonlight in Mayo" and "Biddy Mulligan".
Kavanagh came from the village of Taghmon in County Wexford in the south-east of Ireland and had taken part in the Easter Rising of 1916 and the subsequent War of Independence.
Mooncoin is a small Kilkenny village situated beside the River Suir.
County Kilkenny, the ancient Kingdom of Ossory, has two river boundaries – the River Suir on the south-west and the River Barrow to the south-east. A third large river, the Nore, flows through the centre of the county in a pleasant wooded valley and joins the River Barrow near the point where it begins to widen into its long estuary. On the borders there's some high ground, notably the Slieveardagh and Booley Hills on the County Tipperary border and the hills around Graiguenemenagh near the River Barrow.

Flow on lovely river, flow gently along
By your waters so sweet sounds the lark's merry song
On your green banks I'll wander where first I did join
With you, lovely Molly, the Rose of Mooncoin.

Oh Molly, dear Molly, it breaks my fond heart
To know that we shortly forever must part
I'll think of you Molly while sun and moon shine
On the banks of the Suir that flows down by Mooncoin. *Chorus*

She has sailed far away o'er the dark rolling foam
Far away from the hills of her dear Irish home
Where the fisherman sports with his small boat and line
By the banks of the Suir that flows down by Mooncoin. *Chorus*

Oh then here's to the Suir with its valleys so fair
Where oft times we wandered in the cool morning air
Where the roses are blooming and the lilies entwine
On the banks of the Suir that flows down by Mooncoin. *Chorus*

The Minstrel Boy

Another romantic ballad from the pen of Thomas Moore (1779 – 1852) and set to the old Irish tune "The Moreen".
For further details about Thomas Moore and his songs see the Additional Notes at the front of this book.

The Minstrel fell but the foeman's chain
Could not bring his proud soul under
The harp he loved never spoke again
For he tore its chords asunder
And said "No chains shall sully thee
Thou soul of love and bravery
Thy songs were made for the pure and free
They shall never sound in slavery"

The Minstrel Boy will return we pray
When we hear the news we all will cheer it
The Minstrel Boy will return one day
Torn perhaps in body, not in spirit
Then may he play on his harp in peace
In a world as heav'n intended
For all the bitterness of man must cease
And every battle must be ended.

The Holy Ground

This is a great Irish ballad of the sea, or 'shanty', made famous and popular by a rousing recording of it by The Clancy Brothers. There are two other ballads I've heard of set to the same tune - "Old Swansea Town Once More" and "The Lass of Swansea Town". This ballad is set in the town of Cobh, a fishing village located in Cork Harbour about 8 miles east of Cork city

Cobh was the embarkation point for many Irish men and women emigrating to America

During the period of the Napoleonic Wars (1792 – 1815) Cork Harbour grew in importance as a refuelling and assembly point for naval and commercial shipping. Today Cobh is still the principal Irish port-of-call for transatlantic liners. In 1838 a steamer called "Sirius" left the port of Cobh and became the first to cross the Atlantic, taking 18 days.

On April 11th 1912 the Titanic called into Cobh on her maiden voyage.

The name of Cobh was changed to 'Queenstown' in 1849 to commemorate a visit to Ireland by Queen Victoria but the former name was readopted in 1922.

The name 'The Holy Ground' is given to that part of the town situated on the east side (although there are also rumours that the Hold Ground was a renowned brothel in the town, though I can't get anybody to confirm this!).

When in Cobh you should visit the "Cobh – The Queenstown Story" Visitor Centre, a multimedia exhibition on the origins, history and legacy of Cobh.

A sea shanty is a song sung by sailors while carrying out their tasks at sea. They have distinct and separate rhythms for the various chores performed at sea. Many of the shanties involved a principle singer and a choral response and they served both as a mental diversion and as an aid to synchronised teamwork. Some shanties also provided an outlet for sailors to voice their opinions without the risk of punishment! The main types of shanties were (1) Capstan Shanties, sung by sailors as they marched around the capstan to raise the anchor, (2) Halyard Shanties, sung by sailors as they raised and lowered the sails. This could be very heavy work and usually the crew would rest during the verse and haul during the chorus, (3) Short Drag Shanties, sung by sailors during heavy duty work, (4) Windlass and Pumping Shanties. The windlass was a pumping apparatus used on some ships to raise the anchor. Manual water pumps were also fitted to most ships. These types of shanty were sung to the rhythm of the pump action.

If you're heading off on a sea journey somewhere there's no need for you to learn a bunch of sea shanties. They tell me that computers and electronic gadgets now do all of the work!

For more information on sea shanties, check out the internet site "www.shanty.org".

And now the storm is raging and we are far from the shore
And the night is dark and dreary and our happy thoughts no more
And the good ship she is tossed about and the rigging is all torn
But still I live in hope to see the Holy Ground once more, FINE GIRL YOU ARE! *Chorus*

And now the storm is over and we are safe and well
We will go into a public house and we'll eat and drink our fill
And we'll drink strong ale and porter and make the rafters roar
And when our money is all spent we'll go to sea once more, FINE GIRL YOU ARE! *Chorus*

~~~~~~~~~~~~~~

Love Is Teasing

Marianne Faithful sings a lovely version of this ballad on The Chieftain's album "The Long Black Veil".

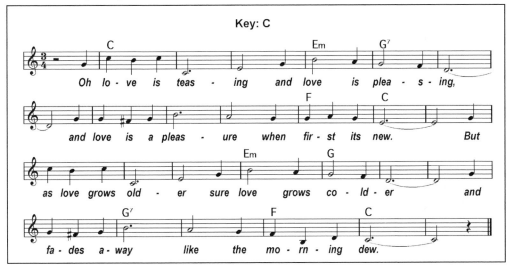

I left my father, I left my mother; I left all my sisters and brothers too
I left all my friends and my own relations; I left them all for to follow you. *Chorus*

And love and porter make a young man older; and love and whiskey make an old man grey
What cannot be cured, love, must be endured, love; and now I am bound for Americay. *Chorus*

The sweetest apple is soonest rotten; the hottest love is the soonest cold
What cannot be cured, love, must be endured, love; and now I am bound for Americay. *Chorus*

I wish, I wish, I wish in vain; I wish that I was a maid again
But a maid again I can never be; till apples grow on an ivy tree. *Chorus*

The Croppy Boy

This song was written by William McBurney, a native of County Down, under the pseudonym of 'Carroll Malone'. It was first published in 'The Nation' newspaper in 1845, without an air. The air and lyrics were first published together in "National Songs of Ireland" edited by M.J. Murphy in 1892.

The air is "Cailín Ó Cois tSiúre Mé" ("I Am The Girl From The River Suir Side"). This air can be traced back to 1584 under the phonetic "Calino Casturame" and is mentioned in Shakespeare's "Henry V'" (Act IV, Scene IV) when Pistol in his gibberish shouts "Callen o casture me!" to the French soldier.

The rebels who took part in the 1798 Rebellion were known as 'Croppies' on account of their short cropped hair cut in the style of the revolutionaries in France.

There is differing points of view as to whether or not this ballad is based on actual events. In W.J. Fitzpatrick's 'The Sham Squire' there is related an incident which is virtually identical to the story told in this ballad, though whether or not that is based on fact is also open to debate.

There is another popular ballad called "The Croppy Boy" which begins, 'It was early early in the Spring, when small birds tune and thrushes sing', and pre-dates the ballad in this book. In that particular ballad the Croppy Boy is betrayed by his own people.

A "yeoman" was a member of a part-time local force established in 1796. It was composed of men loyal to the English crown and comprised mainly Protestant landowners and merchants. The force gained a reputation for indiscriminate and undisciplined sectarian violence.

'Ross' (New Ross) and 'Gorey' are towns which saw scenes of fierce fighting during the 1798 Rebellion. Passage is a town in Waterford where the Croppy Boy in the ballad is said to be buried (interestingly, there isn't a graveyard in the town).

Geneva Barracks was located a few miles from Passage overlooking Waterford Harbour. Geneva Barracks was a settlement built by a group of Swiss dissenters who had settled there in 1783. They subsequently abandoned it and the English authorities used it as a detention centre following the 1798 Rebellion – hence the unusual name.

For further information about the 1798 Rebellion see the Additional Notes at the front of this book.

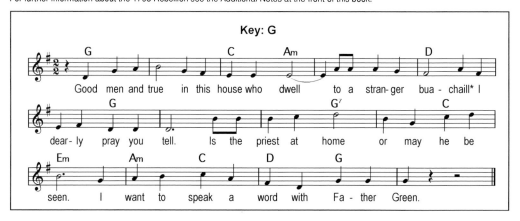

The youth has entered an empty hall, with lonely sounds does his light foot fall
And the gloomy chamber is cold and bare, with a vested priest in a lonely chair.

The youth has knelt to tell his sins; "Nomine Dei" the youth begins
At "mea culpa" he beats his breast; in broken murmurs he speaks the rest.

"At the siege of Ross did my father fall, and at Gorey my loving brothers all
I alone am left of my name and race; I will go to Wexford to take their place".

"I cursed three times since last Easter Day; at Mass-time once I went to play
I passed the churchyard one day in haste and forgot to pray for my mother's rest".

"I bear no hate against living things, but I love my country above my King
Now father bless me and let me go, to die if God has ordained it so".

The priest said naught, but a rustling noise made the youth look up in a wild surprise
The robes were off and in scarlet there sat a Yeoman captain with a fiery glare.

With fiery glare and with fury hoarse, instead of a blessing he breathed a curse
"'Twas a good thought, boy, to come here and shrive, for one short hour is your time to live".

"Upon yon river three tenders float; the priest is in one if he's not shot
We hold this house for our lord and King, and amen say I, may all traitors swing".

At Geneva Barracks that young man died and at Passage they have his body laid
Good people who live in peace and joy, now breath a prayer for the croppy boy.

*Pronounced "voukill" (boy)

~ ~ ~ ~ ~ ~ ~ ~ ~ ~ ~ ~

I'll Tell Me Ma

Belfast city is situated on the north east coast of Ireland and is the capital city of Northern Ireland

Albert Mooney says he loves her; all the boys are fighting for her
They rap at the door and they ring at the bell saying "O my true love are you well"
Out she comes as white as snow; rings on her fingers bells on her toes
Jenny Murray says she'll die if she doesn't get the fella with the roving eye

Let the wind and the rain and the hail blow high and the snow come tumbling from the sky
She's as nice as apple pie and she'll get her own lad by and by
When she gets a lad of her own she won't tell her ma when she goes home
But let them all come as they will; it's Albert Mooney she loves still
(Repeat first verse)

Joe Hill

This ballad is not of Irish origin but is a 'regular' at any Irish ballad session. It was written by the poet Alfred Hayes in 1925.

Joe Hill was born in Gavle, Sweden in 1879. His real name was Joel Emmanuel Haggland and he was one of a family of eight children whose father, Olof, was a railway worker. Life was tough in the Haggland family and deteriorated considerably when Olof died shortly after Joel's eighth birthday. In 1902 Joel decided to emigrate to America to make his fortune. Soon after his arrival in America with his brother Paul, Joel headed off to travel that vast land.

Sometime between 1906 and 1910 he changed his name to Joseph Hillstrom. In 1910 he joined a militant labour movement called the 'Industrial Workers of the World' and at that time changed his name to Joe Hill. During subsequent years he was an ardent labour activist in the front lines of many workers demonstrations.

Hill had a keen love of music and was self-taught on the piano, guitar and violin. He wrote many songs aimed at firing up the poorest of America's workers and several of these songs became 'labour anthems' during the militant labour demonstrations at the time. Throughout this period of worker unrest Hill was under close observation by the authorities.

Hill arrived in Salt Lake City, Utah in the summer of 1913. On the night of January 10th 1914 there was an attempted robbery at a small grocery store and the two raiders shot dead the owner of the store, John Morrison and his son, Arling. During the gun battle it appeared that one of the raiders had also been shot.

At 11.00pm on the same night Joe Hill called to Doctor Frank McHugh with a bulletwound in his chest. He told the doctor that he had been shot during a row over a woman. While in the doctor's surgery a gun dropped from Hill's clothing. McHugh later said that he didn't get a good look at the gun as it was in its holster. After treatment a friend of the doctor's drove Hill home. On the journey Hill asked the driver to stop the car and Hill then apparently threw a gun into a nearby field.

When Doctor McHugh read of the raid on the Morrison grocery he contacted the police and Joe Hill was arrested. Pleading poverty Hill acted as his own lawyer during the preliminary hearing. During the trial itself (at which Hill was represented by two young Salt Lake City lawyers) it was assumed that Hill would testify in his own defence and explain the circumstances surrounding his gunshot wound and perhaps identify the 'woman' he had mentioned to Doctor McHugh. However, Hill refused to testify and speculation continues to this day as to why he made this decision. Acrimony also arose between Hill and his lawyers

On dubious identification evidence Hill was found guilty of murder and was sentenced to death.

Almost immediately his case became a 'cause celebre' for the Industrial Workers of the World who claimed that Hill's conviction was orchestrated by 'Big Business'. Workers' rallies were held throughout America and Hill himself claimed that he had been denied a fair trial. In one of his last messages from his death row cell Joe Hill sent a telegram to his comrade "Big Bill" Haywood. The message would emerge as a rallying cry for downtrodden workers for many years – "Don't waste time mourning. Organise!"

Joe Hill was executed by firing squad on the morning of November 19th, 1915.

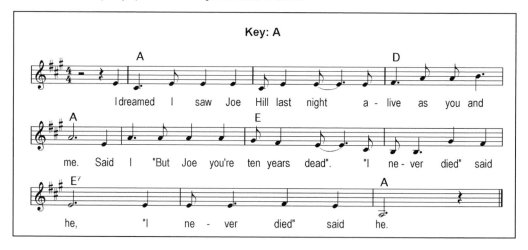

"In Salt Lake City, Joe", said I, him standing by my side
"They framed you on a murder charge". Said Joe "I never died"
Said Joe "I never died".

"The copper bosses shot you, Joe; they filled you full of lead"
"Takes more than guns to kill a man" said Joe, "and I ain't dead"
Said Joe "and I ain't dead".

And there he stood as large as life and smiling with his eyes
Said Joe "what they forgot to kill went on to organise
Went on the organise".

From San Diego up to Maine in every mine and mill
Where working men defend their rights it's there you'll find Joe Hill
It's there you'll find Joe Hill.

(Repeat first verse)

~~~~~~~~~~~~~~

The Last Rose Of Summer

This ballad was written by the great Irish songwriter, Thomas Moore (1779 – 1852).
It was set to the old Irish air "The Young Man's Dream" which was also known as "The Groves Of Blarney".
For further details about Thomas Moore and his songs see the Additional Notes at the front of this book.

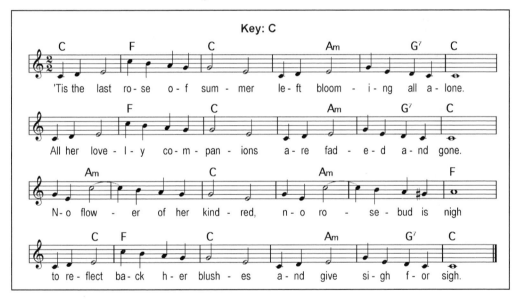

I'll not leave thee, thou alone one, to pine on the stem
Since the lovely are sleeping go sleep, thou, with them
Thus kindly I scatter thy leaves o'er the bed
Where thy mates of the garden lie scentless and dead.

So soon may I follow when friendships decay
And from love's shining circle the gems drop away
When true hearts lie withered and fond ones are flown
Oh who would inhabit this bleak world alone!

The West's Awake

This ballad was written by Thomas Davis (1814 – 1845) to the old Irish air "The Brink of the White Rock". Davis was born in Mallow, Co. Cork. The son of an English army surgeon and Irish Protestant mother he was educated at Trinity College Dublin. The ballad, along with many others written by Davis, reflects the aspiration of the Young Ireland movement of the 1840's of which he was leader. Davis espoused many of his thoughts and ideas for Irish Nationhood in 'The Nation', a weekly newspaper which he founded in October 1842. He also sought to awaken a sense of Irish nationalistic sentiment and pride among Irish people through the many ballads published in 'The Nation', this being one of them. He also wrote another ballad in this book, "A Nation Once Again" (page 98). Davis sought to introduce a new concept to the writing of Irish 'national' ballads. Prior to 'The Nation' most ballads were written as spontaneous and emotional reactions to events and circumstances as they occurred. Davis was determined to utilise the Irish ballad as an instrument to enable and encourage Irish people to reflect on the principle of Irish nationhood. In 'The Nation' of 11th March 1843 he wrote "We furnish political songs to stimulate flagging zeal, or create it where it does not exist".

The best of the ballads printed in the first six months of 'The Nation' were published in a booklet in May 1843 under the title "The Spirit of the Nation, by Writers of The Nation Newspaper". A second booklet was published in November 1843. Both titles were phenomenal successes. 'The Nation' was suppressed by the British administration in 1848 and was revived again by a colleague of Davis, Charles Gavan Duffy, in 1849. It continued until 1897.

Davis died suddenly in September 1845 from an attack of scarlet fever at the age of 31 years.

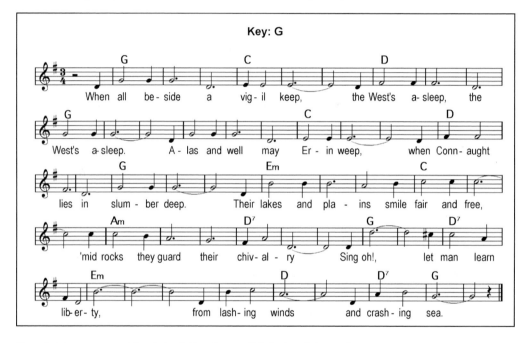

That chainless wave and lovely land; Freedom and Nationhood demand
Be sure the great God never planned; for trodden slaves a home so grand
For long a proud and haughty race; honoured and sentinelled the place
Sing, Oh! Not e'en their sons' disgrace; can quite destroy their glory's trace.

For often in O'Connor's van; to triumph dashed each Connaught clan
As fleet as deer the Normans ran; through Curlew's Pass and Ardrahan
And later times saw deeds so brave; and glory guards Clanricard's grave
Sing, Oh! They died their land to save; at Aughrim's plains and Shannon's wave.

And if when all a vigil keep; the West's asleep, the West's asleep
Alas as well may Erin weep; that Connaught lies in slumber deep
But hark, a voice like thunder spake; the West's awake, the West's awake
Sing, Oh! Hurrah, let England quake; we'll watch till death for Erin's sake.

Carrickfergus

This old and well known ballad acquired renewed popularity through a recent recording of it by Irish singer Van Morrison.
It was originally known as "The Sick Young Lover". The song in its present form may have evolved from two separate songs which would explain why some of the lyrics don't quite make sense. A broadside containing both English and Irish verses was published in Cork in or around 1830. George Petrie in his "Ancient Music Of Ireland" (1855) also publishes a tune called "The Young Lady" which includes many of the words of this ballad.
The town of Carrickfergus in County Antrim stands on the shores of Belfast Lough about 11 miles from Belfast, the capital of Northern Ireland. It is a picturesque port in an old world setting.

My childhood days bring sad reflections of happy times spent long ago
My boyhood friends and my own relations have all passed on now like the melting snow
So I'll spend my days in endless roving; soft is the grass, my bed is free
Ah, to be back now in Carrickfergus, on that long road down to the sea.

Now in Kilkenny, it is reported there are marble stones as black as ink
With gold and silver I would support her but I'll sing no more now till I get a drink
I'm drunk today and I'm seldom sober, a handsome rover from town to town
Ah, but I'm sick now and my days are over, so come all ye young lads and lay me down

Old Maid In The Garret

There are many versions of this popular ballad to be found in Ireland and Britain. One version, with many similarities to this one, was first printed in 1636 and was to be sung to the tune "If 'Be The Dad On't". A later version, entitled "The Old Maid's Last Prayer" was printed around 1825. Another similar ballad entitled "The Poor Auld Maid" was published in 'Folk Songs Of The North-East' (1914).
You'd have to pity the poor unfortunate Annie in the ballad. Nowadays there are singles bars, singles clubs and all sorts of opportunities for women to pursue and ensnare (did I say that?) unsuspecting and innocent men. Indeed a popular and internationally renowned Matchmaking Festival takes place every October in the town of Lisdoonvarna, County Clare.
The Lisdoonvarna Matchmaking Festival is now gaining a reputation in the USA as the best opportunity for a woman to meet up with a real home-grown Irishman with a view to friendship, marriage, etc.

Key: G

I have of-ten heard it said by my fath-er and my moth-er that
go-ing to a wed-ding was the mak-ings of an-oth-er. Well if this be
so then I'll go with-out a bid-ding. Oh it's kind Prov-id-ence, won't you
send me to a wed-ding! For it's oh de-ar me, how will it
be if I die an old maid in the gar - ret!

Oh now there's my sister Jean; she's not handsome nor good-looking
Scarcely sixteen and a fella she was courting
Now she's twenty-four with a son and a daughter
Here am I forty-five and I've never had an offer. *Chorus*

I can cook and I can sew, I can keep the house right tidy
Rise up in the morning and get the breakfast ready
There's nothing in this wide world would make me half so cheery
As a wee fat man who would call me his own dearie. *Chorus*

Oh come landsman or come townsman, come tinker or come tailor
Come fiddler, come dancer, come ploughman or come sailor
Come rich man, come poor man, come fool or come witty
Come any man at all who would marry me for pity. *Chorus*

Oh well I'm away to home for there's nobody heeding
There's nobody heeding to poor old Annie's pleading
For I'm away home to my own wee-bit garret
If I can't get a man then I'll surely get a parrot! *Chorus*

Removal of CD

Carefully cut along the perforated line to remove the CD from the CD case.
Your CD can be stored in this CD case, which is permanently fixed to this
book cover so that you can keep it safely with the book at all times.
Do not attempt to remove the CD case from the cover of the book as it will
result in damage to the book.

www.music-ireland.ie